GEOGRAPHY REVI
FOR JUNIOR CERTI

GEOGRAPHY REVISION FOR JUNIOR CERTIFICATE

3RD EDITION

PATRICK O'DWYER

GILL & MACMILLAN

Gill & Macmillan Ltd
Hume Avenue
Park West
Dublin 12
with associated companies throughout the world
www.gillmacmillan.ie

© Patrick E.F. O'Dwyer 1993, 2000, 2007
© Artwork Gill & Macmillan 1993, 2000, 2007
Design and artwork: Design Image, Dublin
978 0 7171 4124 1
Print origination by Macmillan, India

The paper used in this book is made from the wood pulp of managed forests. For every tree felled, at least one tree is planted, thereby renewing natural resources.

All rights reserved.
No part of this publication may be copied,
reproduced or transmitted in any form or by
any means without written permission of the publishers.
Photocopying any part of this book is illegal.

CONTENTS

1. Maps and Photographs — 1
2. The Earth's Surface — 18
3. Denudation — 27
4. Water — A Natural Resource — 50
5. The Restless Atmosphere — 55
6. Soil — 83
7. Population — 90
8. Settlements — 108
9. Natural Resources — 127
10. Economic Activities — 134
11. Economic Inequality — 148
12. Location Geography — 154

Examination Papers — 160

ACKNOWLEDGEMENTS

For permission to reproduce photographs, grateful acknowledgment is made to the following:

Cambridge University Collection of Air Photographs; Camera Press Ltd; National Meteorological Library (United Kingdom); ESB; Peter Barrow Photography.

CHAPTER 1: MAPS AND PHOTOGRAPHS

GRID REFERENCES ON MAPS

A grid reference is made up of the following parts:

1. **Letter** — It is coloured blue on every map and should be named first.
   L

2. **Eastings** — These are the vertical grid lines. They are numbered at the top and bottom. These should be named second.
   AT

3. **Northings** — These are the horizontal grid lines. They are numbered along the sides. These should be named last.
   AS

HOW TO LOCATE PLACES ON MAPS

Always look across the top first. Then look along the side.

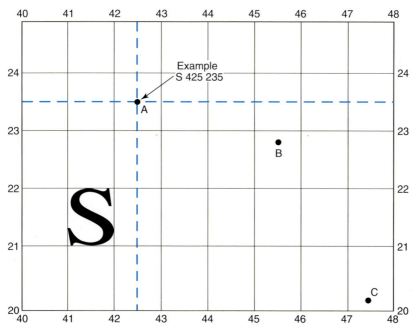

Examples of grid references: A = S 425 235   B = S 455 227   C = S 474 202

1

Maps and Photographs

Remember: **LATAS**
L = Letter
AT = Across the Top
AS = Along the Side

HOW TO LOCATE REGIONS ON MAPS

Four-figure grid references are used to locate a single square on a map. The grid reference used for this purpose is:
- *the sub-zone letter*
- *the easting on the west side of the square*
- *the northing on the south side of the square.*

For example, the Mass Rock is located in region L 70 39; in other words, the bottom left-hand corner of the square.

HOW TO LOCATE MAP REGIONS IN IRELAND

The **national grid** is used to locate places or regions on Ordnance Survey (OS) maps. This national grid **is displayed on the legend** attached to your OS map in an examination. By identifying the **sub-zone** letter on your map you can then identify the location of that region within Ireland.

For example, the sub-zone letter on the map extract at the bottom of page 2 is **S**.
S on the national grid is located in the **south of Ireland**.

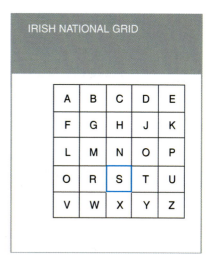

DIRECTIONS ON MAPS

Directions are usually given in the form of compass points. Place a cross representing north, south, east and west on the location you wish to get directions from, for example from Goatstown to Blackwood crossroads (see map on page 4). Then use the compass points to find your answer (*answer : north east*).

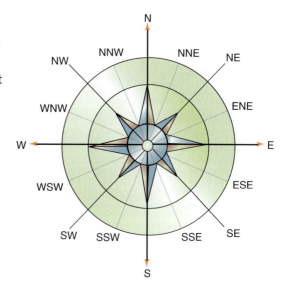

Maps and Photographs

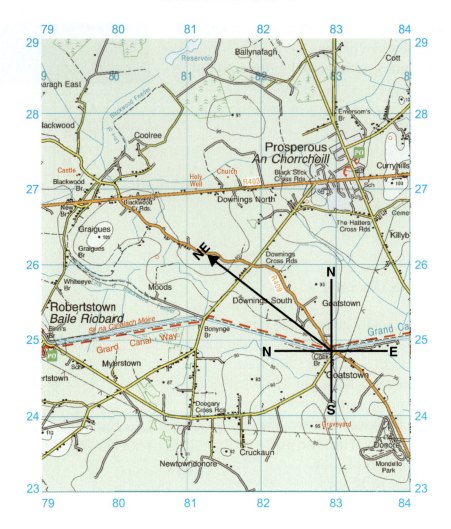

Now identify each of the following directions on this map:

- *from Goatstown to Robertstown*
- *from Goatstown to its nearest graveyard*
- *from Goatstown to Mondello Park*
- *from Blackwood crossroads to Goatstown.*

AREA ON MAPS

To find the area of an OS map:
1. Count the number of grid squares across the top of the region.
2. Count the number of grid squares along the side of the region.
3. Then multiply the number along the side by the number across the top. The area of this map is 2 × 3 = 6 sq km.

To find the area of an irregular-shaped region on an OS map (for example, a water region):
- Count the number of squares that have 50 per cent or more covered by water. Omit all others.
- This number will represent the approximate area of the water region.

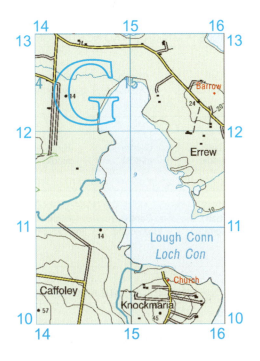

MAPS AND PHOTOGRAPHS

HOW TO LOCATE PLACES ON PHOTOGRAPHS

OBLIQUE PHOTOGRAPH NO NORTH SIGN

Left background	Centre background	Right background
Left middle	Centre middle	Right middle
Left foreground	Centre foreground	Right foreground

OBLIQUE OR VERTICAL WITH NORTH SIGN

North West	North	North East
West	Centre	East
South West	South	South East

N ↑

OBLIQUE OR VERTICAL WITH A NORTH SIGN

North (N ↑)	North East	East
North West	Centre	South East
West	South West	South

DRAWING SKETCH MAPS

- Draw a frame for your sketch map. This frame should be the **same shape** as your **photograph or map**.
- Then draw in guidelines lightly on both the sketch map and the OS map or photograph.

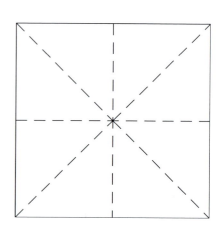

REVISION CHECK LIST

MAPS

Use the check list below to revise maps and photographs.

Scale — straight line measurement, curved line measurement.
Grid references — LATAS: letter; AT — across the top; AS — along the side.
Direction
Area
Cross section
Settlement — density, settlement patterns, functions of settlements.
Description of relief — altitude, slope, highest point, relief features.
Description of drainage — drainage patterns, general drainage of an area, drainage of a particular river.
Communications — different routeways, effects of relief on routeways.
Location of a town — focus of routes, market town, bridging point, defensive site, religious centre, industrial centre, riverside location, altitude of site.
Distribution of woodland — locate woods and forest and account for their location.
Understanding placenames
Sketch maps — be able to draw in the coastline, rivers, lakes, mountain areas, routeways, towns.
Tourism — identify tourist attractions: water sports; historical site; hill walking area; orienteering centre (woodland); beach; golf course; youth hostel; caravan park; camping site.
Planning — justify your choice of site for: a new hospital; a new factory; a holiday village; a new town; a housing estate.

Functions and services of towns.

Choosing a site for industrial development — advantages and disadvantages of a site.
Choosing a site for residential development — advantages and disadvantages of a site.

PHOTOGRAPHS

Locating features
Sketch maps — features and land use.
Explaining the relevance of some features e.g. buildings and architectural styles, street patterns, form and layout of a town.
Understanding street names.
Functions and services of towns.
Building types.
Traffic flow in a town.
Location of original town centre (explain your choice).
Choosing a site for industrial development — advantages and disadvantages of the site.
Choosing a site for residential development — advantages and disadvantages of the site.

DRAWING SKETCH MAPS FROM PHOTOGRAPHS

CASE STUDY: WESTPORT, IN CO. MAYO

Study the photograph of Westport town on page 9. Draw a sketch map (do not trace) of the area shown, and on it mark and label:
- the main streets
- a church
- a car park
- a row of shops
- an industrial or commercial building
- the market square.

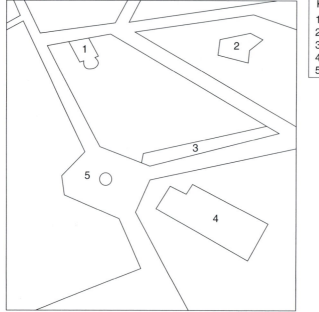

Key (land use)
1. Church
2. Car park
3. Shops
4. Industrial or commercial building
5. Market square

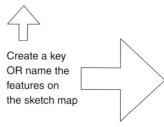

Create a key OR name the features on the sketch map

◀ Sketch map of Westport town

TIPS

1. Always draw a frame similar in shape to that of the map.
2. Never trace a map.
3. Keep the sketch size to less than half of a sheet of A4 paper.
4. Show and name only the features or land uses that you are specifically asked for.
5. Always outline your sketch with a soft pencil. This allows you to correct any errors.
6. Outline features or land-use zones with a heavy boundary line.

Maps and Photographs

Aerial photograph of Westport town

Identify the location of the following letters

A_____   F_____
B_____   G_____
C_____   H_____
D_____   J_____

MAPS AND PHOTOGRAPHS

CASE STUDY: KILRUSH, CO. CLARE

Study the photograph of Kilrush on page 11. Draw a sketch map (do not trace) of the area shown, and on it mark and label:

- the main street
- two other streets
- a church
- an area of housing
- the market square
- a car park.

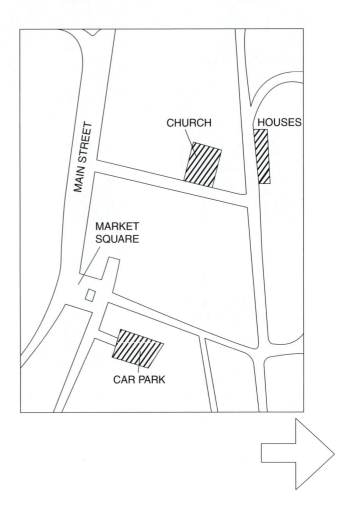

TIPS
- Always use a pencil for your match maps.
- Draw lines lightly at first. Then, when you are sure that each line is correct, mark it with a strong pencil line.
- Name each feature specified.

Maps and Photographs

KILRUSH IN CO. CLARE

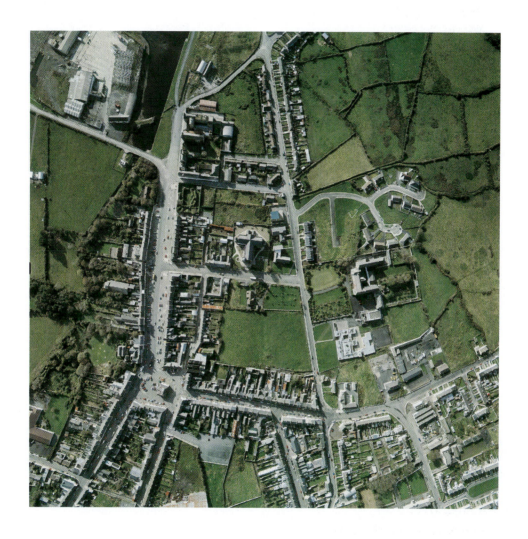

MAPS AND PHOTOGRAPHS

DRAWING SKETCH MAPS FROM ORDNANCE SURVEY MAPS

CASE STUDY: THE NORE VALLEY

Study the map of the Nore Valley on page 13.

1. Always draw a frame similar in shape to that of the map.
2. **Never** trace a map. A sketch map must be drawn freehand.
3. '**Mark**' and '**name**' (or 'label') are different instructions, and marks will be awarded for each separately.
4. Never draw a very large sketch map, as it is more difficult to draw and it takes up too much time.

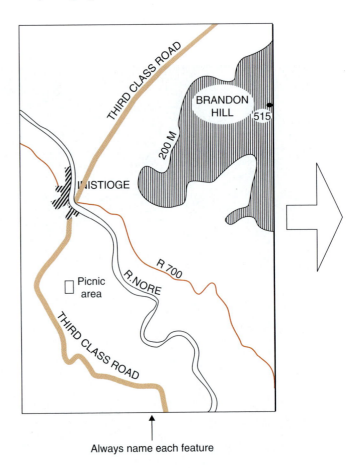

Always name each feature

Draw a sketch map of the Nore River Valley. On it mark and label the following:

- a large river
- one regional road
- two third-class roads
- an area above 200m
- the highest peak
- a picnic site
- an urban area.

Maps and Photographs

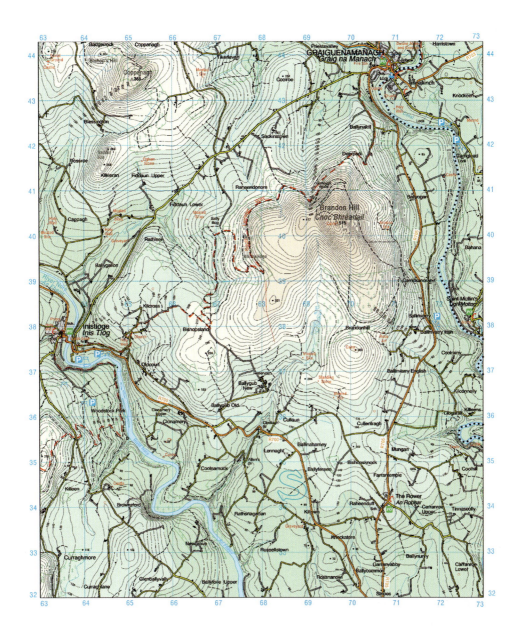

MAPS AND PHOTOGRAPHS

CASE STUDY: SKERRIES REGION

Draw a sketch map of the Skerries region.
Then mark and label the following:

- the coastline
- the urban region of Skerries
- two beaches
- two regional roads
- a railway line
- a railway station
- one island.

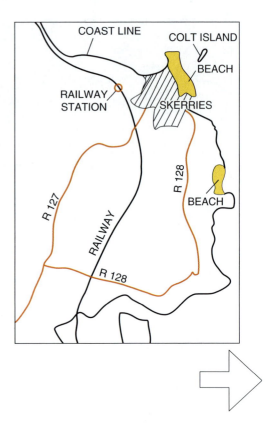

TIPS
- Draw a frame similar to the shape of the map.
- Always mark and name each feature.
- Colour is not necessary.

Maps and Photographs

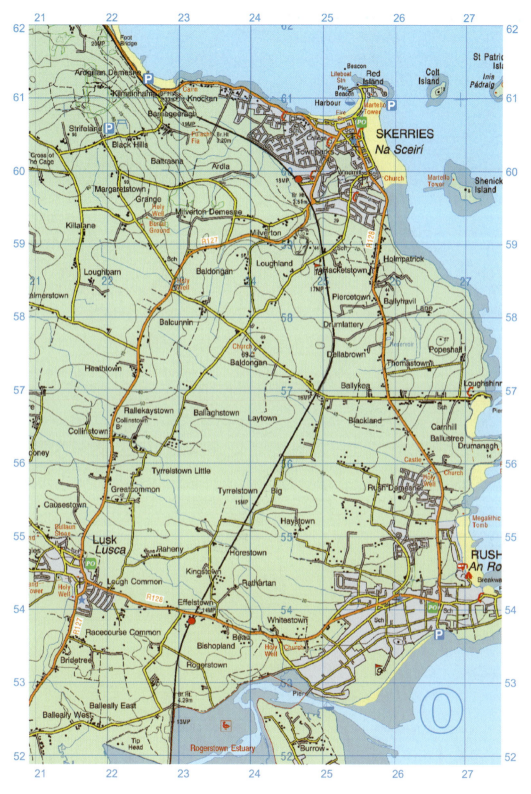

Maps and Photographs

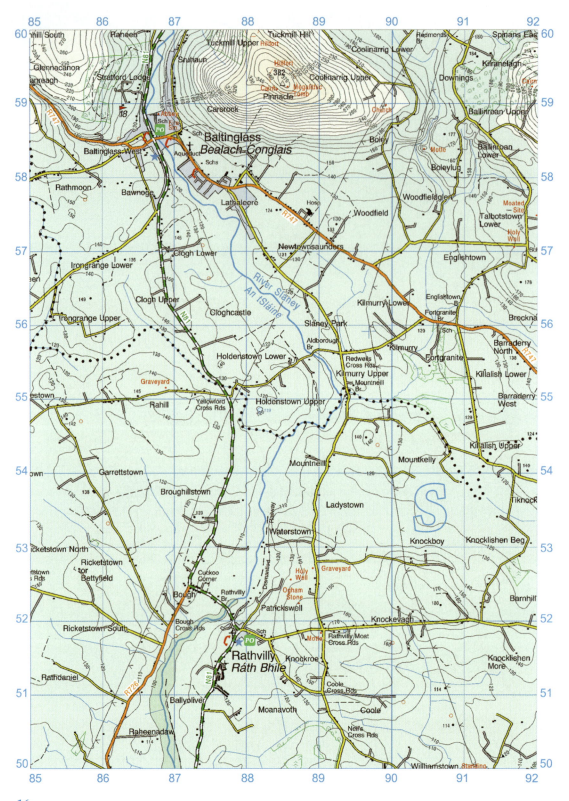

CASE STUDY: SLANEY RIVER VALLEY

Draw a sketch map of the Slaney River valley region. On it mark and label the following:

- two urban regions
- a national secondary road
- two regional roads
- two third-class roads
- a region over 200 metres
- the highest peak.

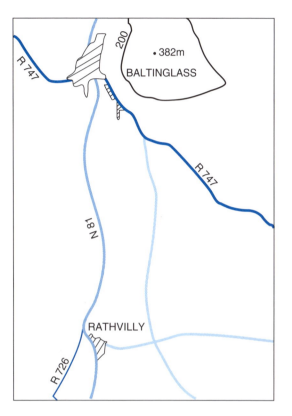

TIPS
1. Always draw a frame similar in shape to that of the map.
2. **Never** trace a map. A sketch map must be drawn freehand.
3. '**Mark**' and '**name**' (or 'label') are different instructions, and marks will be awarded for each separately.
4. Never draw a very large sketch map, as it is more difficult to draw and it takes up too much time.

CHAPTER 2 — THE EARTH'S SURFACE

THE CRUST

Consists of solid rock, mostly basalt and granite.

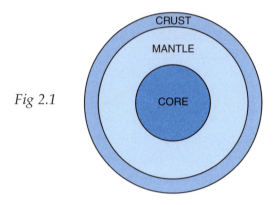

Fig 2.1

THE MANTLE

Consists of heavy rocks. Many of these are in a molten or liquid state because of the very high temperatures (4000°C). Here, rock is so hot that it has melted and flows in slow-moving currents.

THE CORE

This is made up of iron and nickel. It is the hottest part of the earth. Temperatures are greater than 4000°C.

THE PLATES OF THE EARTH'S CRUST

The earth's crust is made up of about 15 pieces or **plates**. These fit together somewhat like a jigsaw. These huge plates float on a heavy semi-molten rock and are moved around by **convection currents** beneath them.

As the plates move around slowly so do the continents and oceans that sit on top of them. This movement of the continents is known as **continental drift**.

In places, these convection currents

   a. drag the plates apart; these are **plates in separation** or
   b. push the plates together; these are **plates in collision**.

The Earth's Surface

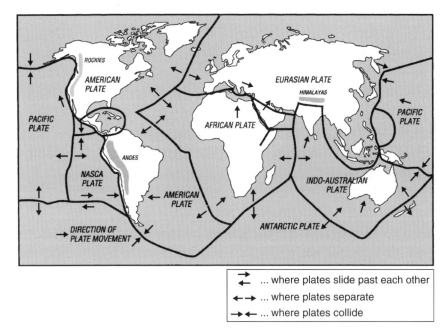

Fig 2.2 Plates of the earth's crust

High mountain ridges occur on the ocean floor in places where plates separate. These are known as **mid-ocean ridges**. Some volcanic islands such as Iceland occur on these mid-ocean ridges.

Fold mountains are found in places where plates collide —

- the Pacific and North American plates collide to form the **Rockies**
- the Nasca and South American plates collide to form the **Andes**.

An **anticline** is an upfold. **A syncline** is a downfold.

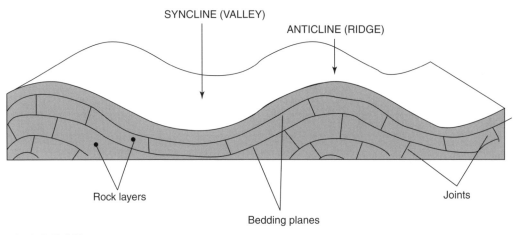

Fig 2.3 Folding

VOLCANOES

Volcanoes and earthquakes occur along zones of collision and separation.

Example: Heimaey in Iceland

FORMATION OF A VOLCANO
1. Hot liquid rock called **magma** reaches the surface of the ground through a narrow vent in the earth's crust.
2. It erupts violently, blasting lava, ash and boiling mud into the air.
3. This material collects around the vent in a cone shape.
4. Repeated lava flows add to this cone-shaped mass of material.
5. Together the repeated ash and lava layers build up to form a cone-shaped mountain.

POSITIVE EFFECTS OF VOLCANOES
1. New land is created for farming and living space e.g. Iceland.
2. Lava soils are rich in minerals. Lava soils grow the finest coffee in the world e.g. Colombia in South America.
3. In Iceland, hot springs called **geysers** are used to heat glasshouses for the production of food.
4. Dormant or extinct volcanoes are major centres of tourism e.g. Vesuvius in Italy.
5. Minerals are created by volcanic activity.

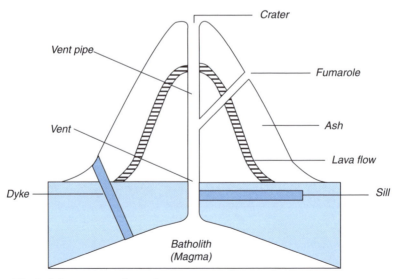

Fig 2.4 Structure of a volcano

NEGATIVE EFFECTS OF VOLCANOES

1. When snow-capped volcanic peaks erupt, large **mud flows** are created which often cover villages and towns.
2. Gases from volcanoes may kill people who live nearby.
3. Ash and lava flows may cover and burn towns causing death.
4. Giant **tidal waves** are created by volcanoes at sea. When they reach land they kill thousands of people, especially in low-lying places such as deltas e.g. Bangladesh.

TYPES OF VOLCANOES

1. **Active** — erupting regularly e.g. Mount St Helens in California, Mount Etna in Sicily.
2. **Dormant** — no eruptions for thousands of years. Vesuvius in Italy covered Pompeii in A.D. 79.
3. **Extinct** — no eruption in recorded history. Derk Hill in Co. Limerick.

EARTHQUAKES

Earthquakes are sudden tremors or vibrations in the earth's crust.

1. Earthquakes occur most often in places where plates collide.
2. Colliding plates build up strain within the earth's crust. The sudden release of this energy causes a violent shaking of the earth's surface.
3. The **focus** is the name given to the place beneath the earth's surface where an earthquake occurs.
4. The **epicentre** is the spot on the surface directly above the focus.
5. Shock waves move out from the epicentre and focus. These shock waves reduce in strength with distance from the epicentre. (The shock waves may be compared to the ripples in a pool when a stone is thrown in the water.)

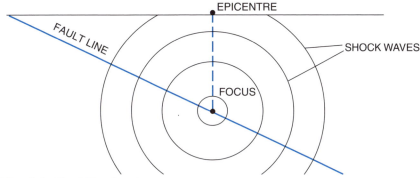

Fig 2.5 Explain the following terms:
*Focus*_____
*Epicentre*_____

6. Greater damage is done to built-up areas close to the epicentre than to places farther away.
7. The lines along which the plates meet are called **fault lines**. The **San Andreas Fault** in California is such an example.
8. **San Francisco** and **Los Angeles** are close to this fault line and so experience earthquakes regularly.

The largest earthquake and volcano zone lies around the edge of the Pacific Ocean. It is called the **Pacific Ring of Fire.**

Ireland is located far from places where plates meet. So it is little affected by earthquakes or volcanoes.

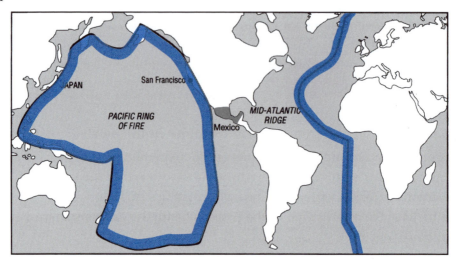

Fig 2.6 The Pacific Ring of Fire and Mid-Atlantic Ridge

DAMAGE CAUSED BY EARTHQUAKES
1. Buildings crumble; cracks appear in walls and ceilings.
2. Bridges and flyovers collapse, often causing death.
3. Railway lines twist.
4. Sewers burst. Escaping sewage may cause disease.
5. Gas mains crack or explode causing death and burns to people.
6. Landslides occur on steep slopes, crushing houses and people, and huge clouds of dust rise into the air.

> A **seismograph** is the instrument used to measure the force of an earthquake. A **tsunami** is a giant wave (tidal wave) caused by an earthquake or a volcano on the ocean floor.

The force of an earthquake is recorded on the **Richter scale.**

ROCK TYPES

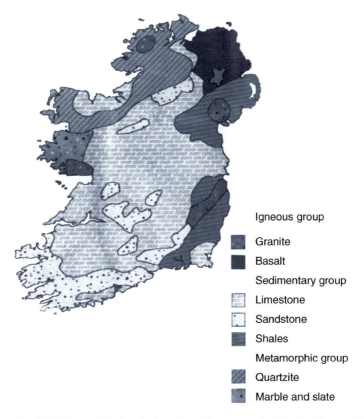

Fig 2.7 Map of Ireland showing the general distribution of the most common rock types

METAMORPHIC ROCKS

Metamorphic means changed under extreme heat or pressure.

When sedimentary or igneous rocks were put under great heat or pressure, they were changed to metamorphic rocks.

Marble

Colour	Green, white, grey or black streaks.
Formation	When limestone was put under great heat or pressure, it turned to marble.
Characteristics	Rough to touch, heavy rock, different colourings, smooth and shiny when polished.
Location	Connemara, Co. Galway; Kilkenny.
Uses	Fireplaces, floors, ornaments, sculpture.

Quartzite

Colour	A light-coloured (whitish) rock.
Formation	When sandstone was put under great heat or pressure, it crystallised to form quartzite.
Characteristics	Very hard rock, rough to touch, smooth when polished. Whitish-grey colour.
Location	Twelve Bens, Co. Galway; Errigal, Co. Donegal.
Uses	Road surfacing.

Fig 2.8 Marble

Fig 2.9 Quartzite

IGNEOUS ROCKS

Basalt

Colour	Dark grey or light brown.
Formation	Magma cooled fast near to the earth's surface.
Characteristics	Heavy rock; found in columns and cubes.
Location	Giant's Causeway in Co. Antrim; Pallasgreen in East Limerick.
Uses	Building construction, filling for roads.

The Earth's Surface

Fig 2.10 Basalt

Granite

Colour	Light brown to speckled black and white.
Formation	Magma cooled slowly deep in the earth's crust.
Characteristics	Shiny specks (crystals), rough to touch, hard rock (may look like a piece of a firelighter).
Location	Wicklow, Donegal, Connemara.
Uses	Building construction, roads.

Fig 2.11 Granite

SEDIMENTARY ROCKS

Limestone

Colour	Light grey to dark grey.
Formation	Formed of tiny marine life which accumulated on the floor of a shallow sea. Their bodies had a calcium carbonate structure.
Characteristics	Heavy, hard fossils, smooth, fine-grained, dissolved by rainwater, forms karst scenery.
Location	Burren, Co. Clare; midlands of Ireland.
Uses	Concrete blocks, roads, cut stone for building.

Fig 2.12 Limestone pavement

Sandstone

Colour	Light brown to dark red.
Formation	When huge amounts of sand accumulate in a large depression or desert, the bottom layers are compressed into rock or, if layers of sand are subsequently covered by other heavy deposits, they are compressed to rock.
Characteristics	Heavy, fine-grained, smooth.
Location	Cork and Kerry Mountains.
Uses	Roads, building construction.

RESOURCES FROM ROCKS

Clay	Used to make building bricks.
	Used to make cement.
Cement and limestone	Used to make concrete blocks.
Coal	Used as a fuel in homes.
	Used as a source of energy to generate electricity.
Iron ore	Used as a raw material to make iron and steel.

METHODS OF MINING

Shaft mining, open cast mining, strip mining.

FUEL-PROVIDING ROCKS IN IRELAND

Coal	Arigna and Ballingarry.
Peat	Bog of Allen and Achill in Co. Mayo.
Natural gas	Off the Old Head of Kinsale.
Oil	Celtic Sea and Porcupine Bank.

CHAPTER 3 DENUDATION

WEATHERING AND EROSION

EROSION

Erosion is the **breaking down** of rock and the **carrying away** of rock particles by moving water, moving ice and wind. It involves the erosion, transporting and depositing of rock particles.

WEATHERING

Weathering is the breaking down of rocks. There are two types, **mechanical** and **chemical.**

Agents of mechanical weathering
1. Frost
2. Sudden temperature change
3. Plants and animals

Agent of chemical weathering
1. Rain

FROST ACTION

In high mountain areas where rain falls, water collects in cracks in rocks by day. At night, the temperature drops and the water freezes and expands, so splitting the rocks. On steep slopes, this loose rock falls downslope and collects as loose heaps of rock. This is known as **scree.**

> Examples: Macgillycuddy's Reeks and the Alps

CHEMICAL WEATHERING

1. Rain passing through the atmosphere joins with carbon dioxide to form a weak carbonic acid ($H_2O + CO_2 \rightarrow H_2CO_3$).
2. This acid dissolves limestone.
3. Limestone is permeable and so allows rainwater to pass through its vertical joints and bedding planes.
4. In this way, limestone pavement (**grikes** and **clints**) are formed on the surface.
5. **Caverns, stalactites, stalagmites, pillars,** and **curtains** and **passages** are formed underground.

Denudation

CASE STUDY: THE BURREN IN CO. CLARE

Definitions

Cavern A large underground chamber in a limestone region dissolved by rainwater.

Stalactite A slender column of calcite which hangs from a cavern ceiling.

Stalagmite A thick column of calcite which forms on a cavern floor directly underneath a stalactite.

Pillar A column of calcite in a limestone cavern formed when a stalactite and a stalagmite join together.

Curtain A continuous sheet of calcite formed when rainwater drips from a fissure in a cavern roof.

Passages Long tunnels formed by underground streams.

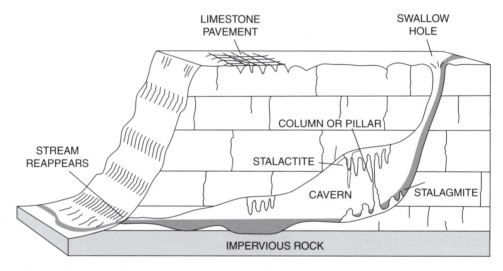

Fig 3.1 Features of a limestone region

BURREN ATTRACTIONS

1. Tourists admire the bleak karst landscape with its unspoilt scenery e.g. Mullaghmore.
2. Geographers study and admire the rock formations e.g. limestone pavement.
3. Historians examine the ancient settlements in the Burren e.g. dolmens and forts.
4. Botanists study the many rare Alpine flowers e.g. gentian.

> **HIGHER COURSE ONLY**
>
> In tropical areas, heavy rainfall, high temperatures and decaying vegetation have rotted the rock to depths as great as 60 metres e.g. Zaire Basin in Africa and Amazon Basin in South America. This weathered rock forms **red** coloured **laterite soils**.

ACID RAIN

People contribute to chemical weathering by creating **acid rain**.

1. When fossil fuels such as coal, peat and oil are burned in industry and homes, gases such as sulphur dioxide and nitrogen oxide are released into the air.
2. These gases join with rainwater to form acids (nitric acid or sulphuric acid), which fall as acid rain.

DAMAGE CAUSED BY ACID RAIN

1. Limestone is dissolved at a much faster rate than normal.
2. Buildings made of limestone are badly damaged e.g. the Acropolis in Greece.
3. Toxic metals are leached from the ground and contaminate water supplies.
4. Lakes are filled with acid rainfall and so will not support fish life.
5. Conifer trees suffer needle loss, root damage and bark injuries and often die.
6. Crop yields are reduced.

WAYS TO PREVENT ACID RAIN

1. Reduce the use of fossil fuels.
2. Increase the use of clean fuels such as electricity, wind power, solar power.
3. Use 'Scrubbers' in chimney flues to extract toxic gases.
4. Insulate houses to reduce fuel consumption.

MASS MOVEMENT

Regolith Loose material weathered from the earth's surface.
Mass movement The downslope movement of weathered material due to the pull of gravity.

FACTORS WHICH AFFECT MASS MOVEMENT
1. High water content causes landslides and mud flows.
2. Vegetation, such as trees, reduces mass movement.
3. Steep slopes aid fast mass movement.
4. Man's interference may aid or restrict mass movement: (aid) removal of trees on steep slopes; (restrict) planting of trees on slopes.

TYPES OF MASS MOVEMENT

Avalanches A very rapid downslope movement of snow or ice on a mountain side.

Landslide A rapid downslope of movement of loose soil and rock. This may occur due to:
(a) A road cutting into a steep slope which may cause regolith above the road to become unstable and fall downslope;
(b) Constant erosion by waves causing undercutting of cliffs. Overhanging ledges collapse downwards as a landslide.

Earth flows and mud flows These occur when soil and mud become saturated by water on steep slopes. This water may result from heavy rain or snow melt after a volcanic eruption.
Example: 1985, Colombia, 20,000 killed as a result of a mud flow.

Bog bursts Occur in mountain bogs of Ireland after periods of heavy rain. Saturated peat moves quickly down slope.

EVIDENCE OF SLOW MOVEMENT
1. Bending of tree trunks.
2. ESB poles tilted.
3. Fencing poles tilted.
4. Bulging or burst walls at the foot of steep slopes.
5. **Terracettes** (like steps) appear on steep grassy slopes in fields.

> *Notice*
>
> When answering questions on physical geography in exams, students should use the term FEED to help them with their answers:
> F — Feature
> E — Example
> E — Explanation
> D — Diagram

THE WORK OF RIVERS

Definitions

Source — The place where a river begins.
Tributary — A river which joins a larger one.
Confluence — The place where rivers join.
Mouth — The place where a river enters a sea or lake.
Estuary — That part of a river's course which is tidal.
Basin — The entire area drained by a river and its tributaries.
Watershed — The high ground which separates one river basin from another.

STAGES IN A RIVER'S COURSE

Young or Youthful Stage; Mature Stage; Old Stage. Otherwise known as Upper Course; Middle Course; Lower Course.

Features of a Young Valley (Upper Course)

1. V-shaped valley
2. Interlocking spurs
3. Waterfalls
4. Rapids

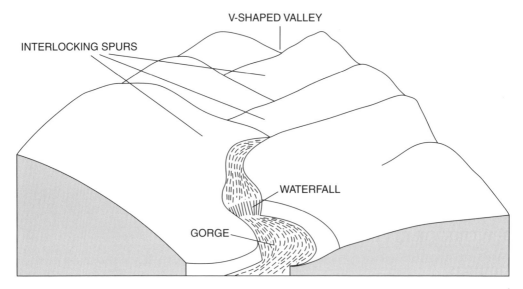

Fig 3.2 Some features of a young river valley

Features of a Mature Valley (Middle Course)

1. Flood plain
2. Meanders

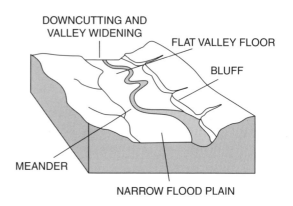

Fig 3.3 Mature valley

Features of an Old Valley (Lower Course)

1. Wide flood plain
2. Ox-bow lake
3. Delta
4. Levee

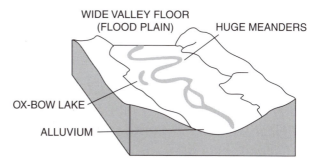

Fig 3.4 Old valley

FEATURES OF RIVER EROSION

V-shaped Valley

Formation

1. A V-shaped valley has steep sides and a narrow floor.
2. Vertical erosion by the river deepens the valley floor.
3. Weathering and gravity causes material to be worn away and tumble down the valley side.
4. The river carries the material away in suspension.

Waterfall

Formation

1. A band of hard rock lies across the river's bed.
2. The river erodes the soft rock downstream from the hard rock.
3. A sudden drop occurs downstream from the hard rock where the soft rock was worn away.
4. The river plunges over this drop to create a waterfall.

Interlocking Spurs

Formation

1. These are projections of high ground which interlock. They project from both sides of a valley.
2. Flowing water is forced to flow around obstacles of hard rock. When this happens, erosion occurs on the outside of a bend. In this way interlocking spurs are formed.

FEATURES OF RIVER DEPOSITION

Flood Plain

A flood plain is a level stretch of land found on both sides of a river in its mature and old stages.

Formation

1. During times of heavy rain, a river's level rises and its speed increases.
2. The swollen river carries large amounts of fine material in suspension.
3. The river overflows its banks and deposits its load.
4. Each time this occurs a thin layer of fine material is laid down on both sides of the river.
5. This fine material is called **alluvium** and deep deposits build up to form a level plain called a flood plain.

Ox-Bow Lake

An ox-bow lake is a horseshoe lake found on the flood plain of a river in its old stage.

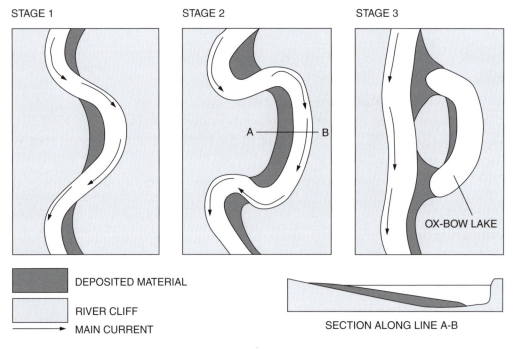

Fig 3.5 *Stages in the development of an ox-bow lake*

Formation

1. A river slows down in its lower stages. This causes it to swing from side to side and form meanders.
2. Meanders may form a loop so that only a narrow neck of land separates their outer banks.
3. In heavy flood the river cuts through this neck leaving the loop as a cut-off.
4. River deposits seal up the cut-off from the river, forming an ox-bow lake.

PEOPLE INTERFERE WITH RIVERS BY BUILDING DAMS

Advantages of Dams

1. Hydro-electricity is generated by turbines.
2. Reservoirs created behind the dams are used by cities and towns as water supplies.
3. Reservoirs are lakes which may be used for leisure activities such as fishing and water sports.

Disadvantages of Dams

1. Reservoir lakes flood valuable farmland.
2. People may be moved to other places as their homes are flooded.
3. Fish, such as salmon, and other animals may be threatened if their natural habitat is changed.

RIVERS INTERFERE WITH PEOPLE BY FLOODING

Flood Damage

1. Towns, villages and individual houses may be flooded when rivers overflow their banks.
2. Crops such as cereals and hay may be damaged on flood plains.
3. People may drown e.g. Bangladesh.

ADVANTAGES OF RIVER VALLEYS TO PEOPLE

1. Flood plains are used to grow crops and rear animals for food supply.
2. Level land in valleys is used for the building of towns and cities.
3. Early settlers used riverside sites for water supply, food supply and transport facilities on the river.
4. Norman settlers used rivers as a mode of defence around their castles.
5. Shallow places in rivers were used as crossing points. Most of our towns and cities developed at crossing points.

Denudation

> *Notice:* Select either moving ice or the sea for study

THE WORK OF ICE

Definitions

Glacier	A river of ice.
Glaciated valley	A steep-sided and flat-floored valley (U-shaped) formed by the action of a glacier.
Crevasse	A long, narrow and deep crack in the surface of a glacier.
Fjord	A glaciated valley which has been drowned by sea water.
Erratic	A large boulder which was carried a long distance from its place of origin.
Outwash plain	A large, gently sloping area of sand and gravel. This material was dropped by streams which flowed from the front of an ice-sheet.
Overflow channel	A V-shaped valley cut by water which flowed from an ice dammed lake.
Pyramidal peak	A peak formed when three or more cirques were located back to back. It was pointed by frost action e.g. Carrauntoohill, Co. Kerry.
Arete	A knife-edged ridge formed when two cirques formed side by side.

PROCESSES OF EROSION BY ICE

Plucking

1. Ice at the bottom of a glacier may melt into the rock over which it moves.
2. This water freezes and shatters rock on the ground.
3. When the ice moves forward it plucks pieces of rock from the ground and carries them away.

Abrasion

1. Loose rock is plucked from the ground by moving ice.
2. The moving ice uses it to scour and smooth the surface over which it passes.

FEATURES OF GLACIAL EROSION
Cirque, arete, U-shaped valley, ribbon lake, hanging valley.

Cirque
A cirque is an amphitheatre-shaped (basin-shaped) hollow in a mountain. It has three steep sides. It may contain a lake.

Formation

Snow collected in mountain hollows and compressed the bottom layers to ice. The ice is rotated and by plucking and abrasion it eroded a deep circular hollow. Sometimes water collects in these hollows to form lakes.

> Example: Devil's Punch Bowl in Co. Kerry

Glaciated Valley
Tongues of ice moved through river valleys during the Ice Age. By plucking and abrasion, the glaciers deepened and straightened the valleys. As glaciated valleys have vertical sides and flat floors they are called U-shaped valleys.

> Example: Glendalough in Co. Wicklow

FEATURES OF GLACIATED VALLEYS
Hanging Valleys
Hanging valleys are also glaciated valleys. They are tributary valleys which hang into the main valley from a higher level.

Formation

Large glaciated valleys were overdeepened by tongues of ice. Tributary valleys had smaller glaciers. So the tributary valleys were not eroded as deeply as the main valley and were left perched at a higher level.

> Example: Glendalough in Co. Wicklow

Ribbon Lake
A ribbon lake is a long, narrow and deep lake on the floor of a glaciated valley.

Formation

Glaciers eroded patches of softer rock from valley floors. Hollows were formed in this way and later filled with water when the ice melted at the end of the Ice Age.

> Example: Glendalough in Co. Wicklow

Denudation

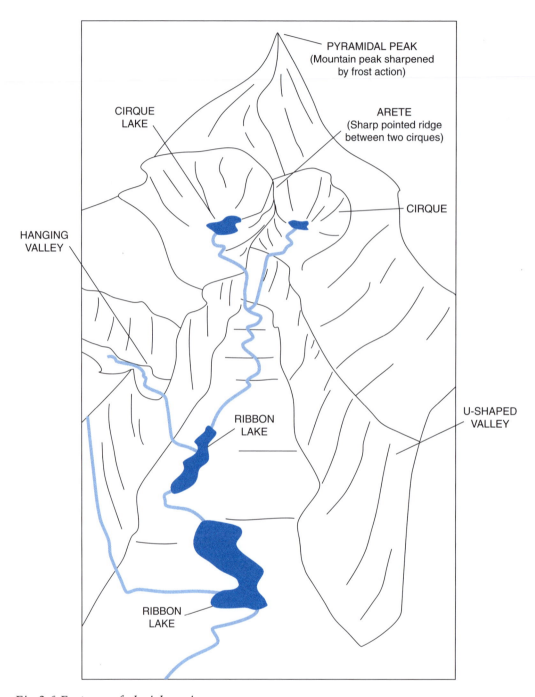

Fig 3.6 Features of glacial erosion

SOME FEATURES OF GLACIAL DEPOSITION
Moraine
Moraine is unsorted material laid down by a glacier or an ice-sheet.

Types of Moraine
Lateral, medial, terminal.

Formation

Lateral moraine is a sloping ridge of unsorted material found along the edge of a glacial valley. Material fell from hill slopes and gathered at the sides of moving glaciers.

Medial moraine is a ridge of unsorted material found along the centre of a glaciated valley. When two glaciers met, their lateral moraines joined to form a medial moraine.

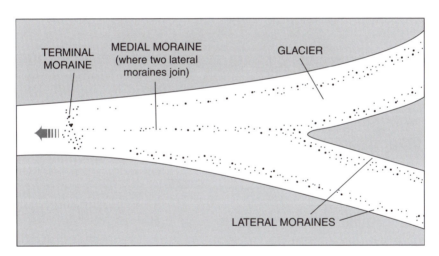

Fig 3.7 Moraine

Terminal moraine is a crescent-shaped ridge of unsorted material found at the entrance to a glaciated valley. Material gathered here along the front of the ice at the point where the glacier stopped and melted.

Drumlins

A drumlin is a low oval-shaped hill up to 60 metres in height. It has a steep slope on the side that the glacier came from.

Formation

It is formed of boulder clay which was deposited by a moving ice-sheet. Drumlins are generally found together in large numbers (swarms). This is called 'basket of eggs' landscape.

Example: Clew Bay, Co. Mayo

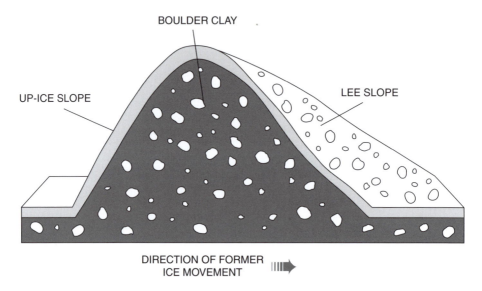

Fig 3.8 Drumlin

DENUDATION

Eskers

An esker is a long, narrow and winding ridge of sand and gravel up to 30 metres high.

Formation

Meltwater flowed through winding tunnels underneath ice-sheets. Large amounts of sand and gravel were deposited on the beds of these streams. When the ice-sheets melted, these beds were left as ridges on the surrounding plain.

Example: Clonmacnoise, Co. Westmeath

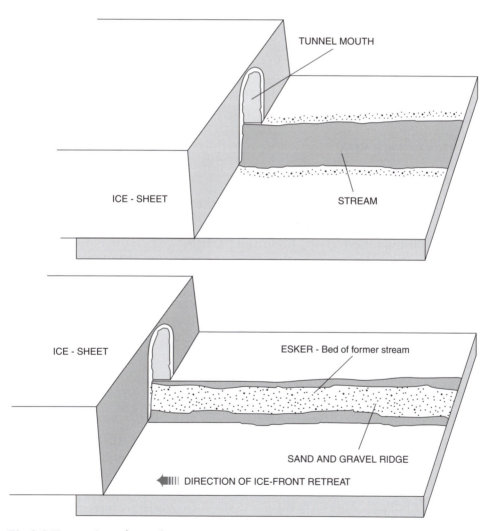

Fig 3.9 Formation of an esker

VALUE OF GLACIATION TO PEOPLE

1. Glaciated regions with their U-shaped valleys and lakes attract tourists to mountain areas e.g. Killarney and Connemara.
2. Fertile boulder clay soils produce high crop yields e.g. Counties Kilkenny and Tipperary.
3. Eskers provide sand and gravel for buildings e.g. Donohill, Co. Tipperary.
4. Glacial lakes are used as reservoirs and sources of hydro-electric power e.g. Blessington Lakes, Co. Wicklow.
5. Glacial valleys provide routeways through mountains e.g. Gap of Dunloe, Co. Kerry.

PROBLEMS CAUSED BY GLACIATION

1. Soil has been stripped from many areas in the west of Ireland e.g. Connemara in Co. Galway.
2. Glacial deposits have caused poor drainage in some areas.

THE WORK OF THE SEA

Definitions

Wave — Wind causes water particles on the surface of the sea to move in a circular motion and form a wave shape. This disturbance is transmitted to neighbouring particles and so the wave shape moves forward (and not the actual water).

Swash — Water which rushes up a beach following the breaking of a wave.

Backwash — The return of the water down the beach.

Longshore drift — The movement of material along the shore.

Load — Mud, sand and shingle carried along the shore by the sea.

SEA EROSION

Sea erosion depends on
a. the strength of the wind,
b. the fetch i.e. the distance of open sea over which the wind blows.

Denudation

The west coast of Ireland is more indented than the east coast. This occurs because erosion is greater on the west coast due to stronger winds and a longer fetch.

WAVES ERODE IN A NUMBER OF WAYS:
1. Hydraulic action. The force or power of the water itself wears away the coastline.
2. Corrasion. During storms, loose rocks at the foot of cliffs are picked up and thrown by the waves against the coast.
3. Compressed air. When waves crash against a cliff, air is trapped in cracks and compressed. When the waves retreat, the escaping air 'explodes' and shatters the rock.
4. Solution. Rocks such as chalk and limestone are dissolved by sea water.

FEATURES OF SEA EROSION
Bay
A bay is a large, curved opening into the coast.

Headland
A headland is a high area of hard rock which just out into the sea.

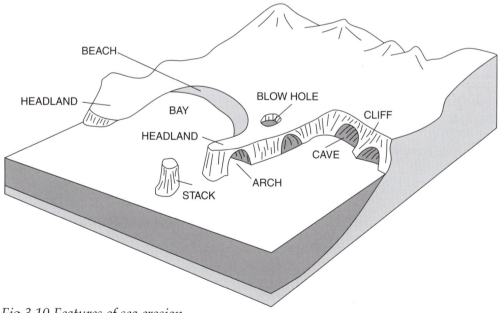

Fig 3.10 Features of sea erosion

Formation

Coastlines consist of areas of hard and soft rock bordering the sea. The soft rock wears away faster than the hard rock to form **bays**. The hard rock juts out to sea on both sides of the bay to form **headlands**.

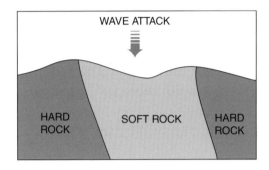
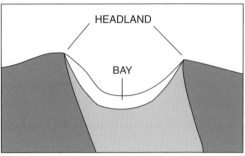

Fig 3.11 Headlands and bay

Sea Cliff

A sea cliff is a steep-sided, high rock face on the coast.

Formation

1. Waves erode a notch in the coast at sea level.
2. Due to undercutting by the waves the notch grows larger.
3. The overhanging rock above the notch becomes unstable and collapses, forming a cliff.
4. A level stretch of rocks forms at the cliff base and is called a **wave-cut platform**.

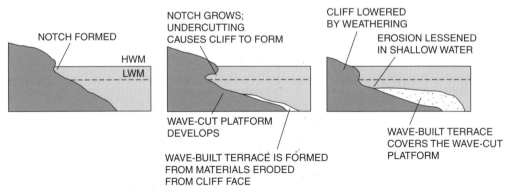

Fig 3.12 Formation of a cliff

Sea Cave

A sea cave is a long, hollow tunnel in a cliff.

Formation

Waves attack and erode a line of weakness or fault in a rock. Hydraulic action and compressed air enlarge the opening until a cave is formed.

Sea Arch

A sea arch is an arch-shaped opening in a rocky headland.

> Example: Old Head of Kinsale, Co. Cork; Bridges of Ross, Co. Clare

Formation

An arch will form when a sea cave erodes straight through a headland or when two caves erode through a headland from either side until they meet.

Sea Stack

A sea stack is a chunk of rock standing up in the sea surrounded by water and unattached to land.

> Example: Cliffs of Moher, Co. Clare

Formation

The roof of a sea arch collapses due to weathering, erosion and the influence of gravity.

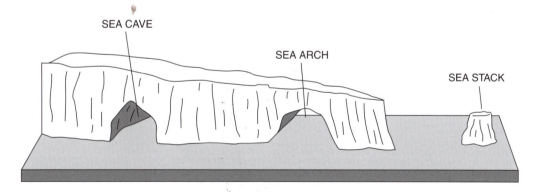

Fig 3.13 Sea caves, sea arch and sea stack

Blow Hole

A blow hole is a funnel-shaped hole which joins a cave to the surface near the cliff edge. During storms, sea spray and white foam are blown up through this hole.

> Example: Bridges of Ross, Co. Clare

Formation

Powerful waves trap air within a cave. When the waves retreat, the released expanding air shatters the rock in the roof of the cave. Eventually, part of the cave roof collapses. That creates an opening to the surface, forming a blow hole.

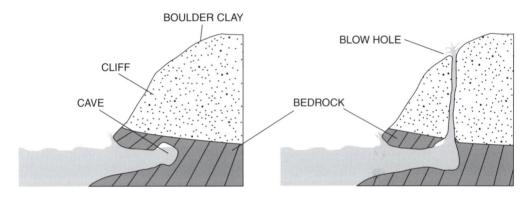

Fig 3.14 Formation of a sea cave and blow hole

TRANSPORT OF MATERIAL ALONG THE SHORE

Longshore Drift

1. Sand and shingle are carried up the shore by the swash at an angle.
2. Each backwash drags some of this material back to sea.
3. In this way, sand and shingle are carried along the shore in a zig-zag manner.

Denudation

FEATURES OF SEA DEPOSITION
Beach

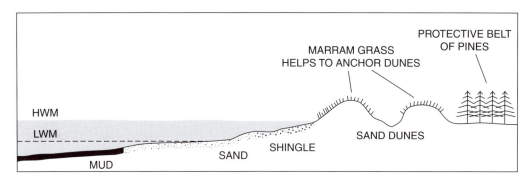

Fig 3.15 Composition of a beach

Example: Bray, Co. Wicklow; Salthill, Galway

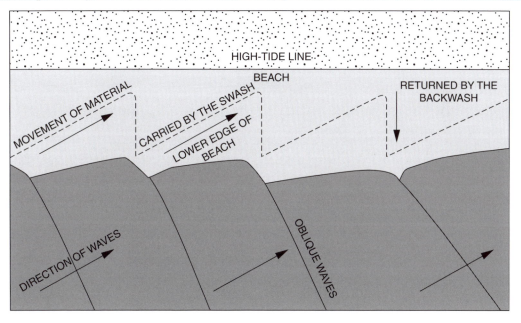

Fig 3.16 Longshore drift and beach formation

Formation
1. A beach is an area of boulders, sand and shingle which is found between high and low tide levels.
2. When waves break they lose their strength and drop the material they are carrying.

3. Sand and shingle are carried up the shore by the swash at an angle.
4. The backwash drags some of this material straight back to sea.
5. Beach material is usually sorted with the largest and heaviest particles at the back of the beach and the finest particles at the water's edge.

Sand Spit

A sand spit is a ridge of sand or shingle which projects out into the sea or across a bay.

Example: Portmarnock, Co. Dublin; Inch strand near Dingle, Co. Kerry

Formation

Longshore drift stops when it is obstructed by a headland or a sheltered place such as a bay. Material builds up over time to form a ridge of sand or shingle.

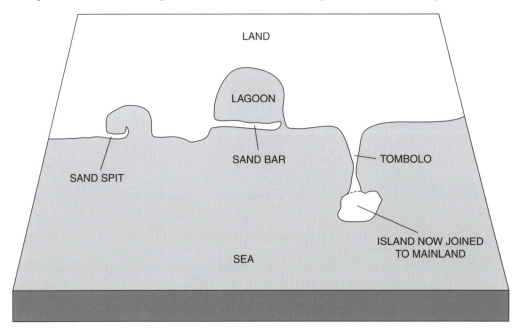

Fig 3.17 Formation of a sand spit, sand bar and tombolo

Sand Bar

A sand bar is a ridge of sand or shingle which builds out across a bay and cuts the bay off from the open sea.

Example: Roonagh Lough, Co. Mayo

Formation

The bar forms when a sand spit grows until it meets the opposite side of the bay and completely cuts the bay off from the open sea.

Tombolo

A tombolo is a ridge of sand or shingle which joins an island to the mainland.

> Example: Near Howth, Co. Dublin; Castlegregory, Co. Kerry

Formation

A sand spit grows until it meets an offshore island and so connects it to the mainland.

PEOPLE AND THE SEA

Ways in Which the Sea is Harmful to People

1. Houses, farmland and roads may be washed away when cliffs are eroded by the waves.
2. Huge waves may flood low-lying areas during storms e.g. the Netherlands.
3. Longshore drift may cause a harbour to fill up with sand and so ships may be unable to continue using it as a port.

To prevent (1) happening, steel pipes are set in the ground to support cliff faces, reinforced concrete walls are built along the cliff face and huge boulders are placed at the foot of the cliff to reduce the force of the waves.

To prevent (2) happening, dykes are built to keep out the sea.

To prevent (3), groynes are built along the coast and dredging of the harbour keeps a deep water channel free for ships.

Ways in Which the Sea is Beneficial to People

1. The sea and beaches provide recreational areas; sunbathing, swimming, sailing, fishing.
2. Large fish catches by trawlers provide food.
3. Large deposits of natural gas have been found e.g. off the Old Head of Kinsale and off the Mayo coast (the Corrib field).
4. Small deposits of oil have been found e.g. off the coast of Waterford.

CHAPTER 4   WATER — A NATURAL RESOURCE

A **natural resource** is something which occurs naturally on earth such as water, minerals and soil.

Water is a renewable resource, which means it can be used again and again if it is cared for properly.

FACTS TO LEARN

1. Water supports human, plant and animal life.
2. People use water for drinking, cooking and washing.
3. Our bodies are formed mainly from water (80%). A person can survive only a few days without water (dehydration).
4. People use water to manufacture many products e.g. concrete, paper, beer.
5. Plants and animals need water. Animals also eat plants and people eat both plants and animals.

So water is a vital resource for people.

Local Water Supply

All parts of the country are supplied with piped water in one of the following ways:

1. by local government supplies (corporation or county council),
2. by private group schemes,
3. by private wells.

Local government and group schemes supply water in the following way:

1. water is collected in a reservoir either from a well or from rivers,
2. water is then filtered, and purified by adding chemicals such as chlorine gas,
3. water is then piped to people's houses.

Example of a reservoir: Pollaphuca, Co. Wicklow

WATER SHORTAGE

DESERTIFICATION

The hot deserts of the world are gradually getting larger and are spreading into neighbouring grassland regions.

Causes
1. Severe droughts have occurred in those parts of the grasslands in Africa that are near to the deserts such as the Sahara. During these long dry spells plants die, soil is exposed, dries out and is blown away by the wind.
2. High birth rates increase the demand for fuel and food. As greater areas are cultivated more soil is exposed to the wind. As trees and shrubs are cut down wind erosion increases and soil is blown away.
3. A greater demand for food leads to overgrazing, soil exhaustion and exposed soil.
4. The best land is owned by wealthy landlords who grow cash crops rather than food crops.

Results
1. Huge areas of agricultural land have been destroyed and turned to desert.
2. Millions of people are forced to leave their homelands and migrate to other areas which in turn become overpopulated.
3. Famines and disease have killed millions of people in countries such as Ethiopia, Sudan and Somalia.

SOLUTIONS TO DESERTIFICATION
1. Shelter belts of trees and coarse grasses are being replanted to bind soil particles together and to reduce the force of the wind along the edges of the deserts.
2. New wells and irrigation methods increase water supplies for grazing land.
3. Numbers of cattle, sheep and goats have been reduced to prevent overgrazing in some areas.
4. Laws are being passed to redistribute the land more fairly and provide training for farmers in more environment-friendly methods of agriculture.

IRRIGATION SCHEME
Definition
Irrigation is the artificial watering of land to aid the growth of crops where otherwise, due to a shortage of rainfall, crops would not grow.

Notice: Choose either the Central Valley Project or the Nile Valley Project for study

THE CENTRAL VALLEY PROJECT IN CALIFORNIA

Reasons for the Scheme
1. California has a Mediterranean-type climate, which means that the region suffers from drought in June, July and August each year.
2. Water supply is plentiful in the north from the Sacramento river, but most of the farmland is in the San Joachin Valley in the south.

Methods of the Project
1. Dams were built on the Sacramento river. Large reservoirs (lakes) were created behind the dams.
2. Canals and aqueducts were built to transfer water from the north to the south of the central valley.
3. Water is stored during the wet winter months for the summer drought.

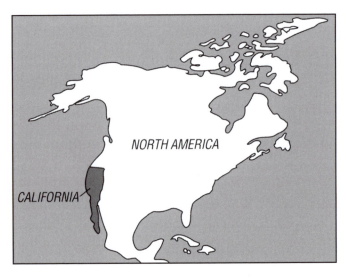

Fig 4.1 California on N. America map

ADVANTAGES OF THE PROJECT
1. Water from reservoirs is used to irrigate land in the San Joachin Valley.
2. Dams are used to generate hydro-electricity.
3. The HEP (hydro-electric power) is used to pump water through the canals and aqueducts to the San Joachin Valley.
4. The San Joachin Valley has changed from a semi-desert area to one that produces cotton, vegetables, lemons, oranges and grapes.

DISADVANTAGES OF THE PROJECT
1. The reservoirs have flooded some farmland behind the dams. Some farmers had to leave their homes.
2. Much water is evaporated from the reservoirs and canals. The remaining irrigation water has a high salt content which poisons the land.
3. Water costs are high which adds to the cost of the crops.
4. Dams were expensive to construct.

OR

THE NILE VALLEY PROJECT IN EGYPT

Reasons for the Scheme
1. To produce more food for Egypt's fast-growing population.
2. To control flooding in the Nile Valley.
3. To store huge amounts of water in one large reservoir to guarantee a reliable supply.
4. To produce more hydro-electric power for industry.

Methods of the Project
1. The Aswan dam, 3.8 kilometres in length, was built across the Nile.
2. A huge reservoir, Lake Nasser, was created behind the dam.
3. Turbines for producing HEP were installed in the dam.

ADVANTAGES OF THE PROJECT
1. Huge amounts of water are stored in Lake Nasser. Water is available all year to farmers along the Nile.
2. Up to three crops can be produced on the same plot each year.
3. Irrigation has increased the amount of land available for growing crops.

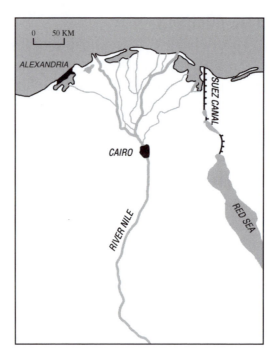

Fig 4.2 The Nile Valley

4. Flooding no longer occurs. Water flow is regulated by the dam.
5. Large amounts of HEP are produced for industries such as aluminium smelting and sugar refining.

DISADVANTAGES OF THE PROJECT

1. Nile farmers must use large amounts of expensive fertiliser on their lands. Fertile silt once carried by flood waters of the Nile is no longer deposited by the river.
2. The Nile delta is being eroded as less silt is carried by the Nile to the sea.
3. Fewer nutrients e.g. plankton are carried by the Nile to the Mediterranean coast. This has reduced fish numbers e.g. sardines so the fishing industry has suffered.

CHAPTER 5 — THE RESTLESS ATMOSPHERE

Definition

The atmosphere (air) is a mixture of gases; nitrogen (78%), oxygen (21%), water vapour, carbon dioxide, ozone and other gases (1%).

HOW THE SUN HEATS THE EARTH

1. The sun's rays pass through the air and strike the earth's surface.
2. These rays heat the earth's surface.
3. The earth's surface then heats the air which is near to it.
4. The warm air rises and much is lost back to space.
5. Some heat remains and this builds up on the earth's surface and in the atmosphere.
6. The sun's rays heat the air unevenly. Vertical rays at the Equator cause great heat while oblique rays at the Poles cause little heat.

The atmosphere is heated in three ways:

1. By radiation. Air close to the ground is heated by heat waves.
2. By convection. Warm air rises.
3. By conduction. Cool air is heated by contact with warm air.

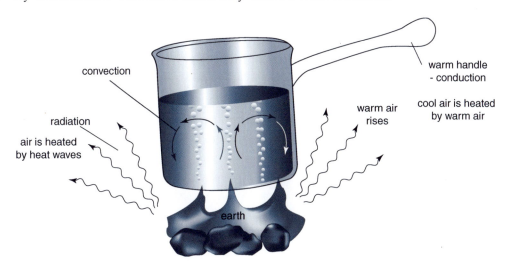

Fig 5.1 Radiation, convection and conduction

THE RESTLESS ATMOSPHERE

Unequal heating of the earth leads to winds and ocean currents.

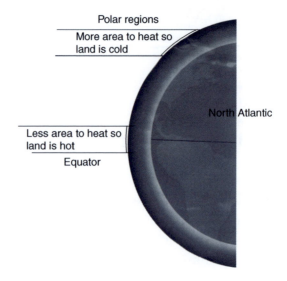

Fig 5.2 Unequal heating of the earth.

WINDS

1. Winds are named after the direction from which they blow.
2. Winds which blow towards the Poles are called **warm** winds. They bring warm air to cool areas.
3. Winds which blow towards the Equator are called **cool** winds. They bring cool air to warm areas.
4. Winds which blow regularly over a region are called **prevailing** winds.
5. Atmospheric pressure means the weight of the air. Heavy air creates areas of high pressure. Light air creates areas of low pressure.
6. Wind is moving air. Air moves from areas of high pressure to areas of low pressure.
7. When air is heated, it expands, gets lighter, it rises and creates low pressure. When air is cooled, it gets heavier, it presses down on the earth's surface and creates high pressure.

8. The rotation of the earth causes winds and ocean currents to be deflected to the right in the Northern Hemisphere and to the left in the Southern Hemisphere. This is called the Coriolis Force effect.

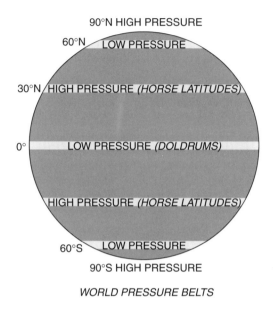

WORLD PRESSURE BELTS

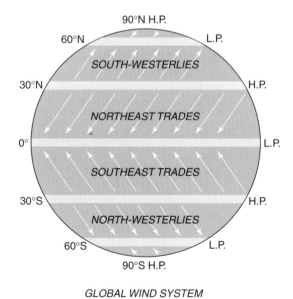

GLOBAL WIND SYSTEM

Fig 5.3 Winds of the world

OCEAN CURRENTS

Ocean currents occur for the following reasons:
1. Unequal heating of the sea at different latitudes. Near the Equator, seas are warm. Warm air expands and is light. Near the Poles seas are cold. Cold water is dense and heavy. These differences cause waters to move between warm sea areas and cold sea areas.
2. Prevailing winds such as the South West Anti-Trades blow the Gulf Stream and the North Atlantic Drift towards Ireland.
3. The rotation of the earth from west to east causes the currents of the Northern Hemisphere to move to the right. This causes a clockwise pattern to occur in the North Atlantic.

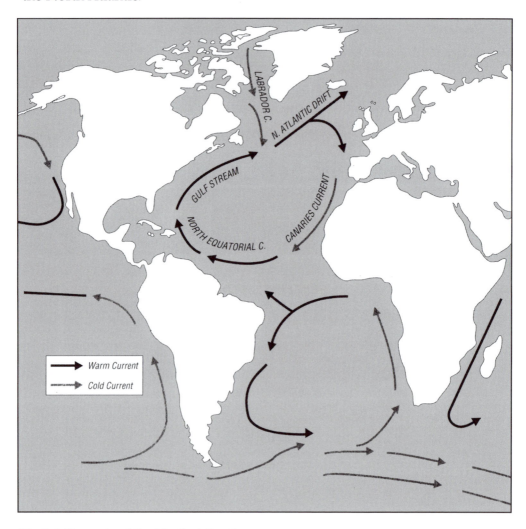

Fig 5.4 Currents of the North Atlantic

The Labrador Current is a cold current in the North Atlantic. It causes the St Lawrence Estuary in Canada to **freeze over** for four months each year.

The North Atlantic Drift is a warm current in the North Atlantic. It causes the waters off the Irish coast to be **ice-free** in winter.

WEATHER AND CLIMATE

Definitions

Weather is the condition of the atmosphere over a short period of time e.g. one day.
Climate is the average condition of the atmosphere over a long period of time e.g. 35 years.
Precipitation is moisture in any form which falls on the earth's surface; rain, hail, snow, sleet, frost and dew.
A **front** is a boundary between two different air masses.

Facts about Ascending Air

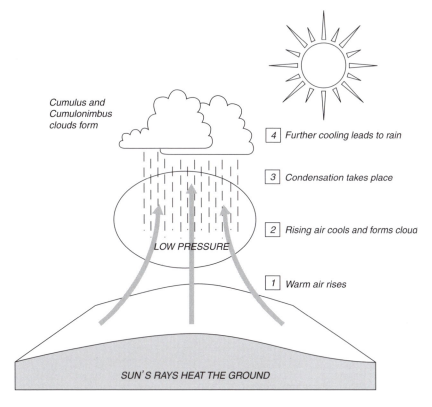

Fig 5.5 Ascending air

1. Warm, light air ascends (rises) creating low pressure.
2. Rising air cools and some of its water vapour is condensed.
3. Condensed air forms cloud. When the air continues to rise it is cooled further and rain falls.
4. Ascending (rising) air forms areas of low pressure. Depressions or cyclones form in low pressure areas.
5. Depressions bring strong, gusting, wet winds.
6. Cloudy, wet conditions are associated with low pressure.

Facts About Descending Air

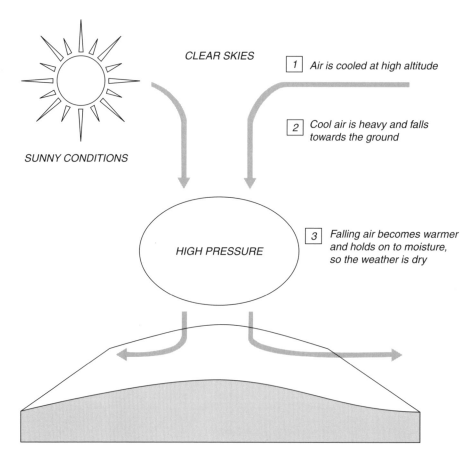

Fig 5.6 Descending air

1. Cool, heavy air descends (falls) creating high pressure.
2. Falling air gets warmer and so is able to hold more moisture.
3. No condensation occurs, so no clouds form and skies are clear.
4. Dry, sunny weather occurs during times of high pressure.
5. An anti-cyclone is an area of high pressure.
6. Calm or slack winds are associated with descending air.

A DEPRESSION IN THE NORTH ATLANTIC

1. Cold, polar air meets warm, tropical air over the North Atlantic.
2. The warm air makes a dent in the cold air mass.
3. The cold air then swirls around the warm air in an anti-clockwise direction.
4. A wedge of warm air called the **warm sector** is surrounded by cold air.
5. This is called a **depression**.
6. Depressions are blown in a northeasterly direction across the Atlantic, bringing rain and changeable weather to Ireland.

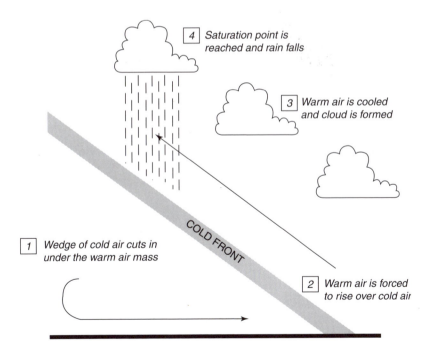

Fig 5.7 Depression in the North Atlantic

THE WATER CYCLE

1. The sun's heat evaporates sea water, forming water vapour.
2. The light water vapour rises high into the air where it cools and condenses, forming cloud.
3. Sea winds blow the clouds inland where they continue to rise, so getting colder, forming rain, hail, snow or sleet.
4. Rivers and ground water return most of the precipitation to the sea. The remainder is evaporated from the land by the sun's heat.

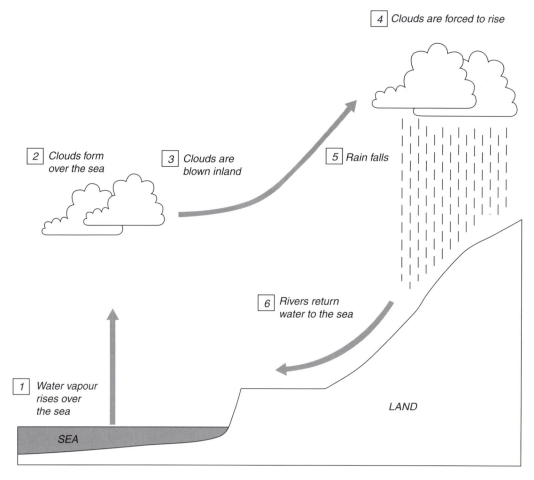

Fig 5.8 The water cycle

RAINFALL

There are three main types of rain — relief rain, convectional rain and cyclonic rain.

RELIEF RAIN

Occurs regularly in the west of Ireland e.g. mountains of Mayo and Kerry.

1. Sea winds are laden with moisture.
2. They are forced to rise over mountains.
3. As they rise, they are cooled.
4. Water vapour condenses and falls as rain on the windward side of the mountain.
5. The leeward or sheltered side of the mountain gets little rain because it is in the rain shadow. As air descends on the leeward side it gets warmer, is able to hold moisture and so is dry.

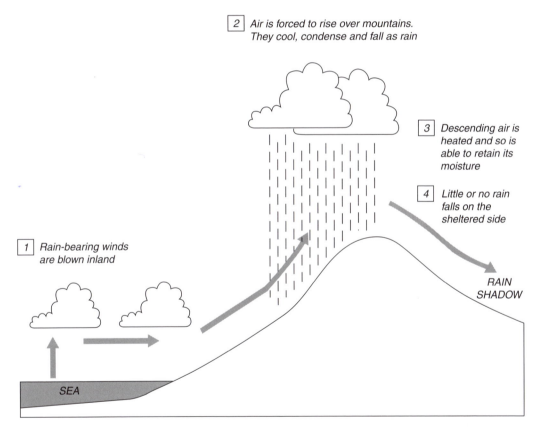

Fig 5.9 Relief rain

CONVECTIONAL RAIN

Occurs regularly at the Equator. It also occurs in summer throughout Ireland.

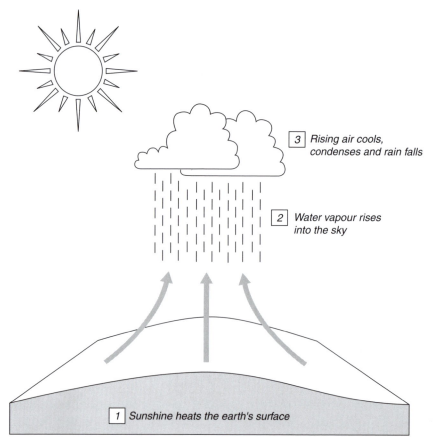

Fig 5.10 Convectional rain

1. The sun heats the ground.
2. The heated air expands, gets lighter and rises quickly.
3. As the air rises it cools, condenses, forms cloud and rain falls.
4. Heavy showers of rain called cloud bursts occur during hot spells.

CYCLONIC RAIN

Occurs regularly in the North Atlantic and Ireland especially in the winter.

1. Cold, polar air meets warm, tropical air over the North Atlantic.
2. The cold air cuts in under the warm air and forces it to rise quickly.
3. As the warm air rises, water vapour condenses and forms cloud along both the warm and cold fronts.
4. Rain falls as showers giving rise to changeable weather.

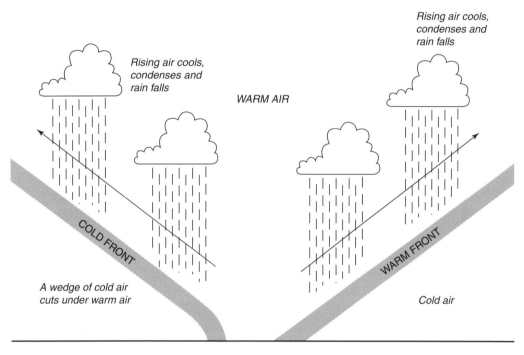

Fig 5.11 Cyclonic rain

IRISH WEATHER

FACTORS WHICH AFFECT IRISH WEATHER

1. No part of Ireland is more than **90 km** from the sea. So the sea has a moderating influence on all parts of the island. Summer temperatures are reduced and winter temperatures are raised.
2. Ireland's prevailing winds (the winds that blow most frequently) are the **Southwest Winds.** They bring both heat and moisture to Ireland and so influence our climate.

3. The warm **North Atlantic Drift** warms the air over it. This warm air is then picked up by the Southwesterlies and brought onshore. This warm air helps keep our shores ice-free in winter.
4. Fronts and depressions move in an east or northeasterly direction across the North Atlantic towards Ireland. These **depressions** bring rain and changeable weather.
5. The western mountains of Kerry, Mayo and Donegal are a barrier for onshore winds. The warm, moist Atlantic air is forced to rise over these **mountains** causing heavy rain.

WORK AT A WEATHER STATION

1. Weather stations observe, measure and record.
2. Information is sent to the central forecasting office.
3. Meteorologists use this information to forecast the weather.

The following are recorded at a weather station.
1. Temperature is recorded by **maximum** and **minimum thermometers**.

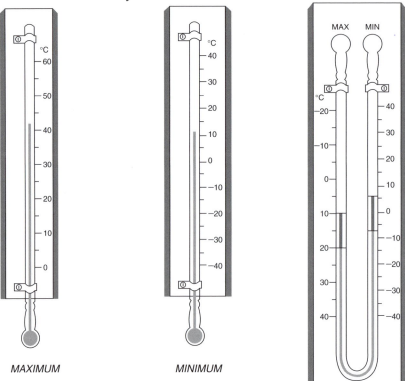

Fig 5.12 Thermometers

The Restless Atmosphere

2. Sunshine is recorded by a **Campbell-Stokes Recorder**.

1. A glass sphere focuses the sun's rays to a pinpoint so that they scorch a removable chart placed behind the sphere

2. Scorch marks on the chart show the length and times of sunshine for the day

Fig 5.13 A Campbell-Stokes Recorder

3. Pressure is recorded by
   (a) a **mercury barometer**;
   (b) an **aneroid barometer**; and
   (c) a **barograph**

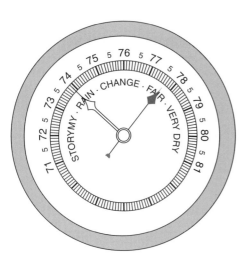

Fig 5.14 Aneroid barometer

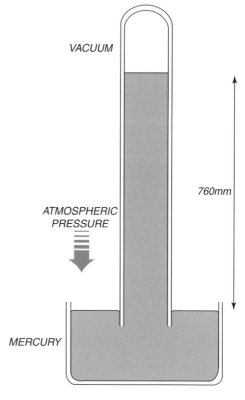

Fig 5.15 Mercury barometer

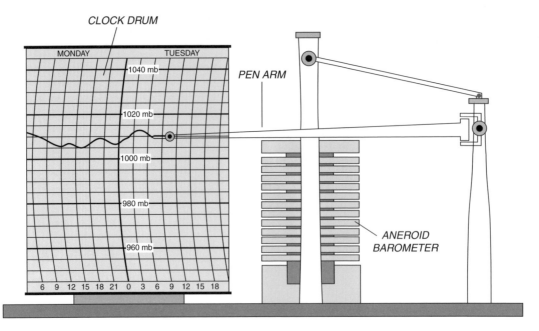

Fig 5.16 A barograph

4. Wind direction is recorded by a **wind vane**.

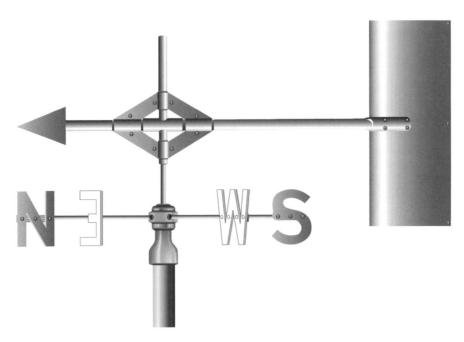

Fig 5.17 Wind vane

5. Wind speed is recorded by an **anemometer**.

Fig 5.18 Anemometer

6. Wind strength is measured by using the **Beaufort Scale**.
7. Rainfall is recorded using a **rain gauge**.

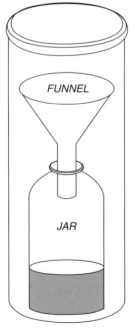

1. Precipitation falling on the funnel is collected in the jar

2. At the same time each day, the contents of the jar are poured into a marked cylinder and recorded

Fig 5.19 A rain gauge

8. Humidity is recorded by a **hygrometer** (a wet and dry bulb thermometer).

Fig 5.20 A hygrometer

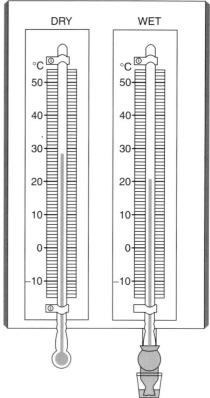

A **Stevenson Screen** is a white, louvred, wooden box in which the following instruments are placed:
1. a maximum and minimum thermometer,
2. a wet and dry bulb thermometer.

Louvred sides for air flow

White colour to reflect sunlight

Fig 5.21 A Stevenson Screen

Definitions

An **isobar** is a line joining places of equal pressure.
An **isotherm** is a line joining places of equal temperature.
An **isohel** is a line joining places of equal sunshine.
An **isohyet** is a line joining places of equal rainfall.

To get:
(a) **mean (average) daily temperature**, add the maximum and minimum temperatures for the day and divide by 2;
(b) **mean monthly temperature**, add the mean daily temperatures for the month and divide by the number of days in that month;
(c) **mean annual temperature**, add the mean monthly temperatures and divide by 12;
(d) **daily temperature range**, maximum temperature of day minus the minimum temperature of day;
(e) **annual temperature range**, temperature of hottest month minus temperature of coldest month.

FACTORS WHICH AFFECT CLIMATE

ALTITUDE
The higher one climbs the colder it gets. 1°C for every 150 metres.

LATITUDE
The nearer to the Equator the warmer it gets; the further from the Equator the colder it gets. The high angle of the sun at the Equator gives greater heat. Days are long near to the Equator and short far away from the Equator.

DISTANCE FROM THE SEA
- The further from the sea the colder in winter and the warmer in summer.
- The sea is warmer than the land in winter so the sea breeze is also warm. In summer, the sea breeze is cool, so reducing summer temperatures near the oceans.

Explanation
- The land surface heats quickly and cools quickly. In summer, continents are hot and in winter they are cold relative to the sea.

- The sea absorbs heat slowly and releases heat slowly. In summer sunlight heats sea water to depths far below the surface and the sea is cool relative to the land.

- In winter it still retains some of this heat and it releases it slowly. So in winter the sea is warm relative to land.

PREVAILING WINDS

If prevailing winds blow from the north they are generally cool and dry. If prevailing winds blow from the south they are generally warm and wet.

OCEAN CURRENTS

Cold currents cause seas to freeze during winter at high latitudes.

> Example: Labrador Current

Warm currents keep seas ice-free in winter at high latitudes.

> Example: North Atlantic Drift

ASPECT

South-facing slopes face the sun and therefore they are warm. North-facing slopes are turned away from the sun and therefore they are cold.

> *Tip*: When describing climate at junior level, always give two pieces of information for both temperature and rainfall.

CLIMATES OF THE WORLD

HOT CLIMATES
Equatorial Climate

> Example: Amazon Basin

Temperature   Hot, 26°C all year. One season.
Rainfall   Wet, convectional rain, thunderstorms, 2000 mm per year.
Vegetation   Selvas. Dense forest with little undergrowth.

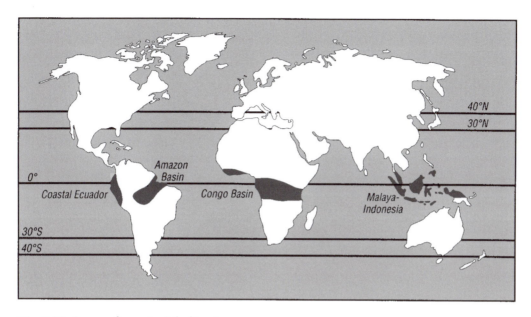

Fig 5.22 Areas of equatorial climate

Savanna Climate

Example: Savanna grassland of Africa

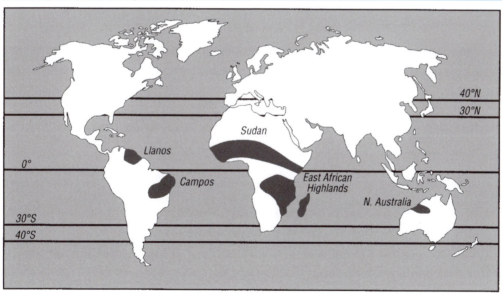

Fig 5.23 Areas of savanna climate

Temperature   Hot, 30°C all year.
Rainfall   **Dry season** for six months. **Wet season** for six months.
Vegetation   Savanna grasslands.

CASE STUDY

HOT DESERT

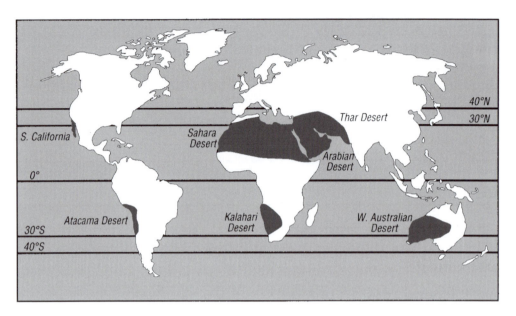

Fig 5.24 Areas of hot desert

Example: Sahara

Temperature
Hot, 30°C all year.

Reasons
1. Hot deserts are located **between 15° and 30° north and south** of the Equator so the sun shines from overhead throughout the year.
2. **Clear skies** cause the ground to reach very high temperatures during the day. However, it gets **bitterly cold at night** as heat escapes due to absence of cloud.

Rainfall
Dry, 0 to 250 mm.

Reasons
1. The **trade winds** blow constantly over the hot deserts.
2. The trade winds blow towards the Equator and as they blow from continents they are dry winds.
3. Some hot deserts are in the rain shadow of high mountains e.g. Kalahari.
4. Cold ocean currents offshore cause winds to lose their moisture at sea. On reaching dry land they are dry winds.

Vegetation
1. Cactus, thorn shrubs, creosote.
2. Date palms, figs.

These plants are adapted to their environment because:

1. Cacti have (a) **sponge inside** for storing water, (b) grooves in the skin to allow them to swell and (c) **needle leaves** to prevent moisture loss.
2. Desert plants have (a) **long roots** which reach deep into the ground for water and (b) **waxy skin** to prevent moisture loss.
3. Lush vegetation and food crops grow where water is close to the surface e.g. at oases.
4. Desert plants survive on soils with little nutrient value.

Animals
Fox, snake, lizard, camel.

Desert People
1. Oasis dwellers
   Some areas of hot deserts have local water supplies e.g. well, water hole or river. People use this water supply to grow crops such as dates, cereals and figs.
2. Nomads
   The Bedouins of Arabia travel from place to place with their animals e.g. sheep and goats. They live in tents.
3. Oil workers
   Recent discoveries of oil have led to oil fields and their associated workers.

TEMPERATE CLIMATES

Cool Temperate Oceanic Climate

Example: Ireland

Temperature   Mild winters 6°C, warm summers 15°C. Small annual range.
Rainfall   Rain all year round. Generally relief or cyclonic. 1000–2000 mm.
Vegetation   Deciduous woodland — ash, oak, chestnut.

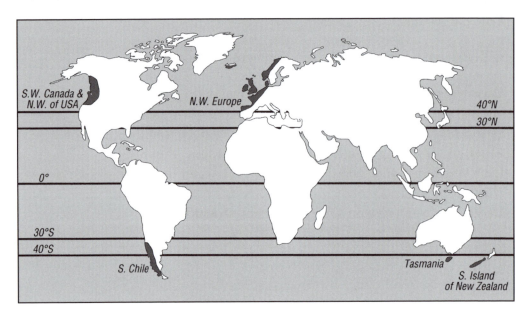

Fig 5.25 Areas of temperate climate

Reasons Why Ireland is an Important Tourist Region
1. Glaciated mountain areas such as Killarney and Glendalough offer rugged mountains, lakes and quiet landscapes for the tourist.
2. River basins e.g. the Shannon offer water sports such as boating, fishing. Spectacular waterfalls such as Powerscourt waterfall attract tourists.
3. The west of Ireland offers unspoilt landscape such as beaches e.g. in Co. Donegal and Co. Clare.
4. Golf courses and sports e.g. rugby offer variety of choice for the tourist.
5. Old cities such as Dublin and Limerick offer museums, educational centres and historic buildings as places of interest.

CASE STUDY

WARM TEMPERATE OCEANIC CLIMATE (MEDITERRANEAN)

Temperature
Hot summers (25°C), warm winters (12°C).

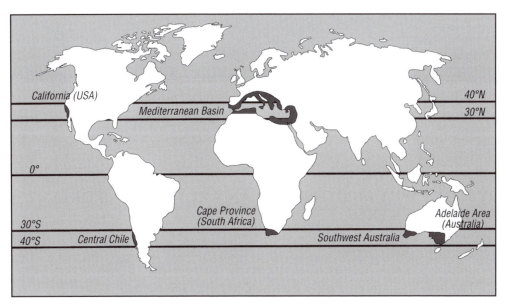

Fig 5.26 Areas of Mediterranean climate

Rainfall
Dry summers (June, July, August), wet winters.

Reasons Why Summers are Hot and Dry
1. The trade winds blow over the Mediterranean areas. As the trade winds come from land areas and blow towards the Equator, they are dry winds.
2. High pressure covers this area in summer. This brings hot, dry, sunny weather.
3. Mediterranean areas are close to the tropics, so it is hot.

Reasons Why Winters are Warm and Wet
1. The Southwesterly Anti-Trades blow over Mediterranean areas. These winds come from the sea and so they are wet.
2. The winds come from a lower latitude and so they are warm winds.

Vegetation
1. Mediterranean woodland, cork oak, chestnut.
2. Sparse scrub-like grass and herbs such as lavender.

Animals
Sheep and goats as they can survive on sparse and poor-quality vegetation.

People
1. Farmers grow vines (for wine and fruit) and citrus fruits e.g. lemons, oranges. They keep sheep and goats for milk and meat.
2. Tourism. Many people are employed in hotels, guesthouses. Others are employed in the construction of accommodation for tourists e.g. hotels, villas, etc.

REASONS WHY MEDITERRANEAN AREAS ARE IMPORTANT TOURIST CENTRES

Example: Benidorm in Spain

1. The hot dry summers offer guaranteed sunshine for tourists.
2. Well-developed facilities such as hotels, restaurants, roads and airports are available.
3. Living costs are relatively low and so families avail of **package holidays**.
4. Golden beaches and warm Mediterranean waters offer a welcome change to people from cooler countries such as Ireland.
5. Famous places such as Roman ruins and cities such as Venice and Rome are focal points for tourists.

Advantages of Tourism
1. Many people are employed in hotels, guesthouses and travel agencies.
2. Industries such as construction expand and prosper.
3. Farmers sell their produce to retailers and direct to tourists so raising their standard of living.
4. Services such as roads, airports, water and sewage works are improved which aid both tourists and local people.
5. Farmers sell their land as development property and so make money.
6. Different nationalities meet and enjoy each other's cultures and languages so reducing barriers and division between peoples.

Disadvantages of Tourism

1. Tourism is seasonal, so many people earn low or no wages for some months during the off-season.
2. Cost of living, especially food and housing, is high for the local population.
3. Services such as water supply are difficult to maintain during the peak season.
4. Once unspoilt beaches are now overlooked by ugly concrete apartment blocks.
5. Land values rise too high to be purchased by locals.
6. Sewage disposal is a major problem. As a result sea areas such as the Mediterranean are polluted.

COLD CLIMATES
Tundra

Temperature   10°C, cool, **short summer**. Long cold winter.
Rainfall   250 mm, **mostly as snow**.
Vegetation   Mosses, lichens, Arctic flowers, dwarf shallow-rooted shrubs.

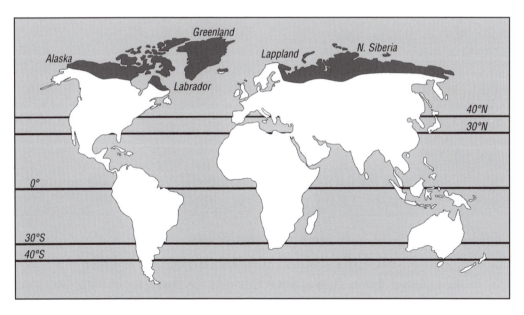

Fig 5.27 Areas of tundra climate

CASE STUDY

BOREAL

Examples: Alaska, Siberia

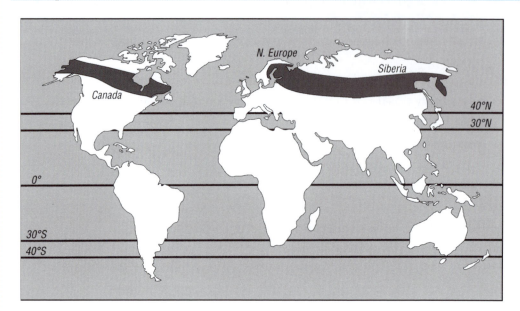

Fig 5.28 Areas of boreal climate

Temperature
Summers short, warm, 16°C; long days. Winters very cold, −25°C; long nights.

Rainfall
Heavy rainfall near the Atlantic and Pacific Oceans. Very little rain falls in places far from the sea. Heavy snowfalls in winter.

Reasons Why Summers are Short and Warm
1. Summers are short as the boreal areas are far from the Equator.
2. In the summer this region is tilted towards the sun, giving long, warm days.

Reasons Why Winters are Long and Cold
1. In winter this region is tilted away from the sun. This causes long nights.
2. Boreal lands are in high latitudes, between 50°N and the Arctic Circle. The sun's rays are at a very low angle and so have little heat.

Vegetation
Coniferous forest e.g. spruce, pine, fir. These conifers are adapted to their environment because:
1. They are cone-shaped which allows heavy snow to slide off.
2. They have needle-shaped leaves which prevent moisture loss in winter.
3. They keep their leaves in winter so they are ready to grow once spring arrives.
4. Conifers grow quickly with straight trunks.
5. The soil has few nutrients, but conifers grow well on poor soil.

Animals
Reindeer, caribou, boar.

People
1. **Lumberjacks.** They cut down the conifer trees with chainsaws. The trunks are cut into short lengths for easy handling. They are lifted on to trucks by machines for transport. They are turned into fuel, pulp, planks and furniture.
2. **Trappers.** They trap animals such as mink and fox for their fur, which they sell.
3. **Miners.** Minerals such as iron ore and oil are extracted from the ground.

CLIMATE CHANGE

THE GREENHOUSE EFFECT

The temperature of the earth's surface and atmosphere is increasing due to a build-up of gases, such as carbon dioxide, which retain heat.

Causes of the Greenhouse Effect

1. Trees absorb carbon dioxide. But the Equatorial forests such as those in Brazil are being cut down and not replaced.
2. The burning of fossil fuels, such as wood, coal and oil, produces large amounts of carbon dioxide. This increases the amount of carbon dioxide in the air and so raises temperature.
3. Carbon dioxide in the air traps heat from the earth and prevents it from escaping out through the atmosphere. This causes a build-up of heat in our atmosphere.

Results of the Greenhouse Effect

1. Increased heat in the atmosphere causes more surface evaporation leading to drought, crop failures and famine in places such as the Sahel in Africa (**desertification**).
2. Polar ice caps are melting causing a rise in sea levels. Flooding of farmland and low-lying cities may result.

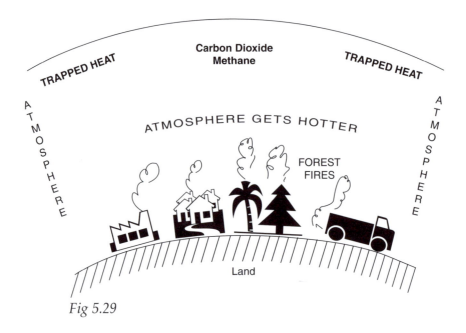

Fig 5.29

CHAPTER 6   SOIL

Soil is a mixture of

(a) **minerals** — the main ingredient,
(b) **humus** — enriches the soil,
(c) **micro-organisms** — break down plant litter,
(d) **air** — adds oxygen,
(e) **water** — dissolves minerals.

SOIL SAMPLE

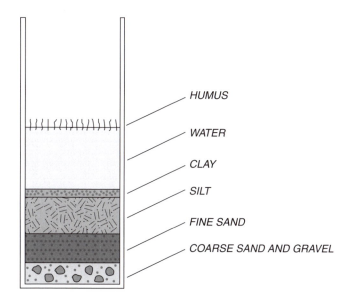

Fig 6.1 Soil sample

IRISH SOIL TYPES

Examples: Podzols and brown soils

SOIL

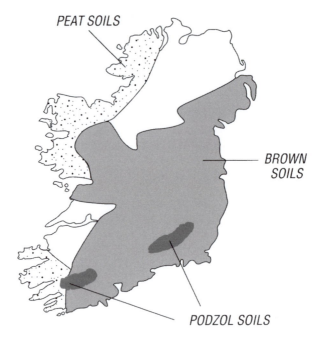

Fig 6.2 Irish soils

PODZOLS
Location
Boggeragh Mountains in West Cork.

Found
1. On the floors of coniferous forest.
2. In heathland.

Reasons for their Distribution
1. Coniferous forest floors are low in humus due to pine needles.
2. Heavy rain causes high leaching. This causes hard pan to form beneath the surface.

Characteristics
1. Grey colour due to an absence of humus.
2. Low in mineral value due to an absence of humus and the presence of leaching.

BROWN SOILS

Location
Midlands of Ireland.

Found
On the floors of deciduous forest or where deciduous forest once grew.

Reasons for their Distribution
1. Decaying deciduous leaves provide a plentiful supply of humus.
2. Brown soils have only moderate rainfall so little leaching occurs.
3. Occur in lowland areas where deciduous forest is found.

Characteristics
1. Dark brown colour.
2. High mineral content due to presence of humus.

Notice: Higher Course only

TROPICAL RED SOIL

Location
Tropical forest regions e.g. Amazon Basin.

Reasons for their Distribution
1. High temperatures and heavy rainfall give rise to intensive chemical weathering so creating very deep soil.
2. Rapid vegetation growth and heavy leaf fall ensure a constant supply of humus.
3. The mineral particles have a high iron content. This gives the soil a red colour.
4. Dense forest cover protects the soil from heavy rain.

PEOPLE INTERFERE WITH TROPICAL RED SOILS IN THE FOLLOWING WAYS:
1. Forests are cleared by machines for agriculture and timber supplies. Soils are exposed to direct heavy rainfall. Soil is leached as there is no leaf fall to maintain nutrients.
2. Trees are cut down on steep slopes. With no tree roots to bind the soil together it is prone to erosion. Much soil is washed into rivers and carried downstream. Soil becomes infertile and exhausted.

Soil

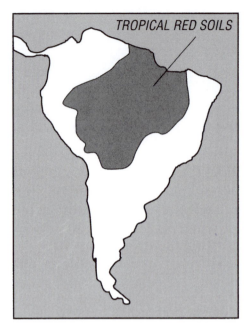

Fig 6.3 Amazon Basin in South America

PEOPLE CAN PREVENT SOIL EROSION IN THE FOLLOWING WAYS:

1. **Terracing.** Steps may be cut into a steep slope. Crops may be grown on these wide steps.
2. **Replanting.** Trees may be replanted to protect the soil and create leaf fall to produce humus.
3. **Contour ploughing and strip cropping.** Hills should be ploughed across the slope to prevent sudden run off. Crops of different kinds should be planted so there is always some vegetation on the hill.
4. **Shelter belts.** Lines of trees help break the force of the wind and so prevent erosion.

SOIL

1. Answer the following questions.

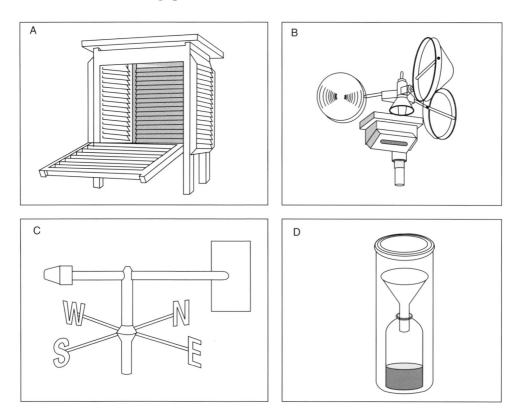

Fig 6.4 Weather instruments

Name the instruments A, B, C, D.
A.. C..
B.. D..

Name three instruments housed in A and state their use in the space provided below.

	Instrument	Use
1.		
2.		
3.		

87

SOIL

2. Underline the correct alternative in each of the following statements:
   1. Depressions are areas of **high/low** pressure.
   2. Anti-cyclones bring **dry/wet** weather to Ireland.
   3. Ireland's climate is **cold temperate/cool temperate oceanic**.
   4. **Isobars/Isotherms** join points that have the same mean temperature.
   5. The sea helps to keep temperature **moderate/extreme**.
   6. The sea keeps Ireland's coastline **cool/warm** in winter.
   7. Ireland's prevailing winds are **Northeasterlies/Southwesterlies**.
   8. The North Atlantic Drift **reduces/increases** summer temperature.

3. Insert one of the following where appropriate: **Cools, vapour, relief, west, east, decreases, shadow, warmed, snow.**
   High ground lying in the path of a wind containing water .... causes .... rain. The ascending air expands and .... producing cloud followed by rain or .... When the air descends on the leeward side it becomes compressed and .... so that rain does not fall. This area is called the rain .... This explains why most rain falls in the .... coast of Ireland and that as one travels .... the amount of rainfall ....

4. Read the passage below and in the spaces provided write the correct words, choosing only **ONE** of the alternatives given:
   Hot deserts are found on the (western/eastern) .... margins of continents. In these regions the (westerly/trade) .... winds blow offshore. These winds blow from (cooler/warmer) .... regions and are able to (hold/impart) .... moisture. Temperatures during the (day/night) .... are very high, but there is a (large/small) .... daily range of temperature partly caused by the (presence/absence) .... of cloud cover.

   In (central/northern) .... Chile the hot desert is called the (Thar/Atacama) .... Desert. The (Sahara/Namib) .... Desert is in southwest Africa. Cultivation is confined to the (terraced slopes/oases) .... where (bananas/cacti) .... flourish. In the Sahara desert the (Bedouins/Pygmies) .... are wanderers.

The Mediterranean climate is also called the (cool/warm) .... temperate (western/eastern) .... margin type of climate. This type of climate is found in (northern/central) .... Chile around (Valparaiso/Antofagasta) .... It is also found in (southern/central) .... California around (La Paz/San Francisco) .... In the Northern Hemisphere the (tropical/hot desert) .... is found immediately to the (north/south) .... of the Mediterranean regions.

The (summer/winter) .... season is dry. Plants are adapted to withstand the drought. Trees have (large/small) .... leaves. The (olive/banana) .... tree is the most characteristic. The (vine/acacia) .... is also cultivated. The chief wine-producing areas of the world are (Holland/France) ...., (Italy/Belgium) .... and (Spain/Sweden) ....

Tundra regions have (long/short) .... summers. The average summer temperature is (10°C/20°C) .... Average annual rainfall is (less than/more than) .... 250 mm. Two regions experiencing the conditions are northern (Canada/Australia) .... and northern (Denmark/Norway) .... In (December/June) .... both of these regions have long days. Vegetation in these regions is (dense/sparse) .... and consists of (lichens/llanos) .... and (mosses/trees) .... Life in these regions is hard. The (Eskimo/Pygmy) .... depends on (lumbering/fishing) .... and (hunting/agriculture) .... for his livelihood. The (Aborigines/Lapps) .... also live in tundra regions.

CHAPTER 7   POPULATION

WORLD POPULATION DISTRIBUTION

SOME AREAS OF HIGH POPULATION DENSITY

1. Eastern and Southern Asia

Examples: India, Japan

Reason

a. Large, fertile river valleys such as the Ganges provide rich alluvial soils which can support a high population.
b. Industrial cities such as Tokyo can support many people. Many jobs and high wages allow for large numbers of people.

2. Western Europe

Examples: France, Germany

Reason

a. Fertile regions such as the Paris Basin can produce many crops such as wheat and barley for food.
b. Industrial centres such as the Ruhr provide employment and high wages for large numbers of people.

SOME AREAS OF LOW POPULATION DENSITY

1. Tundra and Boreal Areas

Reason

a. Cold winters and short summers cause people to avoid such areas.
b. Few crops will grow due to the absence of sufficient heat.

2. Amazon Basin in Brazil

a. The climate is very hot and humid. This makes it difficult and unattractive to work in.
b. Dense jungle and the absence of routeways limited population numbers in the past. Recent migration to the Amazon has increased its population.

THE POPULATION CYCLE

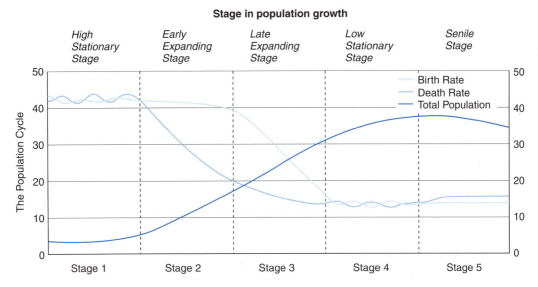

Fig 7.1 The population cycle

1. HIGH STATIONARY STAGE

Small world population. Birth rate is high; death rate is high; population growth is slow.

Reason

Famines, disease and lack of food and medical knowledge keep the death rate high.

2. EARLY EXPANDING STAGE

Birth rate is high; death rate falls rapidly; population growth is rapid.

Reason

The economy of the country begins to develop. Medical and food supplies increase so fewer people die. Therefore the population grows quickly.

3. LATE EXPANDING STAGE

Birth rate is low; death rate is low; population grows but at a slower rate.

Reason

People decide to have smaller families, so population growth slows down.

4. LOW STATIONARY STAGE

Large world population. Birth rate is low; death rate is low; population growth is slow or nil.

Reason

People are prosperous and prefer small families.

5. SENILE STAGE

Birth rate is lower than replacement level. A country's population reduces.

Reason

Educated young couples wish to remain prosperous.

FACTORS AFFECTING POPULATION GROWTH

1. FOOD SUPPLY

When food supplies are absent or low, people die. This food shortage is called a famine. Population falls. When food supplies are in abundance people live longer and population grows.

2. WAR

People die during times of war. During the First and Second World Wars in Europe, millions of people died. In Germany three million people died during World War 1 and four million died during World War 2.

3. IMPROVED TECHNOLOGY

Improved farm machinery has led to greater farm outputs. So food supplies have increased. Improved medical equipment saves many lives.

4. HEALTH
In the past low hygiene standards and lack of medical knowledge caused high death rates. Today improved public health, vaccines and health awareness reduce deaths.

5. EDUCATION
People who are educated are more likely to understand and practise family planning schemes. Educated women often choose careers outside the home. This practice generally leads to smaller families. In Brazil families tend to be large while in Germany families tend to be small.

6. WOMEN IN SOCIETY
In undeveloped and developing parts of the world, women have little say in decision-making. Many marry young and have large families.

In developed countries, women tend to choose careers rather than stay at home. This generally leads to smaller families. Therefore, as women take more control in decision-making, their families tend to be smaller.

FUTURE POPULATION GROWTH
Positive View
Some people believe that as economies develop, population growth will slow down and level off.

Negative View
Some people believe that population growth will continue to rise. This could lead to the world becoming so overcrowded that its resources may be unable to sustain such numbers. So a world famine may result.

IRELAND'S POPULATION TRENDS SINCE 1800

1. 1800–1845 (BEFORE THE FAMINE)
The population in the west of Ireland grew quickly. At this time food was plentiful and the potato was the main diet. There were high birth rates.

2. 1845–1849 (FAMINE YEARS)
The potato crop was destroyed by blight. People in the west of Ireland were worst affected as they depended on the potato alone for food. Over one million died, others fled the country and emigrated to Britain and America.

3. 1849–1960 (AFTER THE FAMINE)

After the Famine and into the twentieth century, Ireland's population continued to decline. People continued to emigrate to countries such as America and Britain. By 1960 Ireland's population had fallen to 3 million.

4. 1960–1980

Many factories offered employment during this period. Emigration stopped and some emigrants returned from Britain. By 1980, Ireland's population had risen to 3.4 million.

5. 1980–1990s

During this period Ireland's population growth slowed down. Many people emigrated to Britain and America once again. This occurred due to factory closures.

6. 1990–PRESENT (CELTIC TIGER)

Ireland's population has grown dramatically. It is now 4.2 million. Many immigrants have come to Ireland. There is full empolyment.

POPULATION DISTRIBUTION IN IRELAND

LOW POPULATION DENSITY

CASE STUDY: THE WEST OF IRELAND

REASONS WHY THE WEST OF IRELAND HAS A LOW POPULATION DENSITY

1. The Famine

The failure of the potato crop in 1845, 1846 and 1847 meant starvation and death for thousands, especially in the west where the potato was the main crop.

2. Repeal of the Corn Laws

Irish farmers changed over to dairy farming and cattle rearing. Pastoral farming does not require as much labour force as arable farming, especially since the introduction of machinery, and so many thousands left the land in search of work.

3. Emigration

At this time Ireland was not industrialised. Many fled the land to seek a better living in Britain, North America or Australia.

4. 1990s to the Present

The population of the west continues to decline for the following reasons:

1. Farms in the west of Ireland are small and unprofitable. People are leaving the land for jobs in the cities.
2. As young people leave the west the services such as schools, recreational centres and hospitals close. The region becomes unattractive to live in.
3. An aged population remains; birth rates fall and so a drop in population results.
4. Industry is reluctant to set up in an area where the work-force is limited.

EFFECTS OF LOW POPULATION IN THE WEST OF IRELAND

1. Low Marriage Rates

The west of Ireland offers few jobs, recreational centres or other social facilities for young people. So most people between the ages of 18 and 30 emigrate from the area. Few marriageable young people remain and so birth rates are low.

2. Abandoning Agricultural Land

The small, difficult and often hilly farms of the west of Ireland offer few prospects for young people today. So they leave the land in the care of older people who often lack the energy to work them fully. Many farms become neglected or abandoned when the older people die.

3. Political and Economic Isolation

The west of Ireland is lightly populated, so its voting power is limited when compared to the densely populated city areas of the east coast. It is also the farthest part of Ireland from the core area of the EU. As a result, it is the least prosperous and most isolated part of Ireland with only a minimum amount of essential services. Industry is reluctant to set up in an area where the work-force is aged and limited.

HIGH POPULATION DENSITY

CASE STUDY: DUBLIN REGION

REASONS WHY DUBLIN REGION HAS A HIGH POPULATION DENSITY

1. Dublin is Ireland's capital city. Company headquarters, the civil service and the Dáil all centre in Dublin.
2. Dublin is Ireland's main industrial centre. Industries such as Guinness and Jacob's, as well as modern industrial estates, offer a wide range of industrial jobs.
3. Dublin is Ireland's main port. Goods are imported and exported to other EU countries through Dublin port.
4. Dublin is Ireland's main educational centre. Colleges and universities such as Trinity College and University College Dublin are located in the city
5. Dublin is a centre of inward migration. Over the past decades, thousands of people from rural Ireland have migrated to Dublin in search of employment.
6. A cluster of dormitory towns has developed around Dublin. Towns such as Malahide are inhabited by commuters, i.e. people who work in the city and travel to work each day.

POPULATION DISTRIBUTION WITHIN BRAZIL

High population density — example, east coast of Brazil.
Low population density — example, the Amazon Basin.

CASE STUDY: EAST COAST OF BRAZIL

SOCIAL AND HISTORICAL REASONS

REASONS WHY THE EAST COAST OF BRAZIL HAS A HIGH POPULATION DENSITY

1. The Portuguese discovered and colonised Brazil. They set up trading towns along the coast. Almost all transport was by sea, so more and more people settled along the coast.

POPULATION

2. Plantations were established close to the coast. These had to be near ports to export sugar and cotton to Europe. Millions of black Africans were brought as slaves to work the plantations. Their descendants make up half of Brazil's population today.
3. Large industrial cities such as Rio de Janeiro and Sao Paulo offered jobs and high living standards. People flocked to these areas and their populations continued to grow.
4. Many people fled from the drought-stricken northeast (the Sertao). They moved to the cities of the east coast in search of employment and food.
5. Up until recent times the hot, wet climate, fear of malaria and the presence of Indian tribes discouraged settlers in the Amazon region.

POPULATION DISTRIBUTION IN SWEDEN

High population density — example, Scania (Southern Sweden).
Low population density — example, Norrland (Northern Sweden).

CASE STUDY: SWEDEN

REASONS WHY SOUTHERN SWEDEN HAS A HIGH POPULATION DENSITY

1. Southern Sweden has a warm climate which allows for the production of many crops for food.
2. Deep boulder clay soils and flat lowland areas are suited to agriculture.
3. Large mineral deposits such as iron and copper give rise to many industries e.g. iron and steel.
4. Large ice-free ports such as Malmo and Goteborg allow the import and export of goods throughout the year.
5. Large cities such as Stockholm are centres of education, recreation and industry.

REASONS WHY NORTHERN SWEDEN HAS A LOW POPULATION DENSITY

1. Norrland is near the Arctic Circle. It is very cold, which limits the growth of crops for food.

2. Infertile thin soils which are frozen for much of the year can support only coniferous trees.
3. Much of the region is elevated and windswept thus making it unsuited to farming or to people.
4. Roads are few, so industry is not attracted to the region.
5. Cities are confined to the shores of the Baltic Sea. Few towns are found inland so people are not attracted to the region.

CONTRASTING POPULATIONS …

Brazil … a rapidly growing population
Germany … a declining population

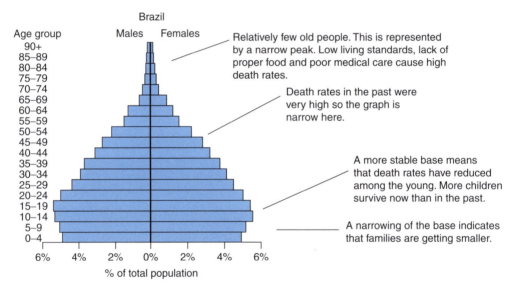

Fig 7.2 Population structure of Brazil

POPULATION

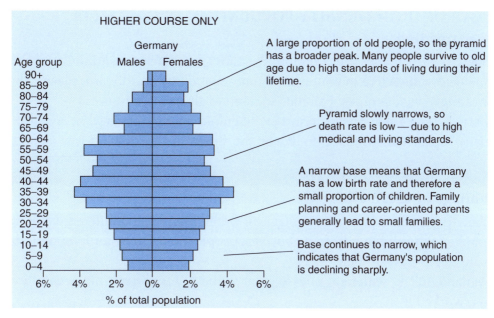

Fig 7.3 Population structure of Germany

REASONS FOR THE RAPID CITY GROWTH IN THE DEVELOPING WORLD

OR

REASONS WHY CALCUTTA HAS GROWN SO RAPIDLY

1. Farmers find it increasingly difficult to support a family on their small farms. Many are poor and hungry and parents feel that cities offer better opportunities than the countryside.
2. Landowners have not invested in their estates so working conditions and incomes have deteriorated over the years. They are forced to leave to seek a better living elsewhere.
3. Urban wages are generally many times higher than those in the countryside. Rural people are lured into the cities on the chance of earning a decent living.
4. Health clinics, hospitals, schools, water supplies and electricity are all available in the cities. Rural areas lack many and sometimes all of these services. The better facilities attract rural migrants to the cities.
5. The young and adventurous people migrate to the cities. They see the cities as places of better opportunities. They may also wish to have a better standard of living than their parents may have had.

Notice: Lower Course students should choose either Calcutta or Hong Kong for study

EFFECTS OF HIGH DENSITY POPULATION IN CALCUTTA

1. Overcrowding
a. Overcrowded homes are common. Families share kitchens and toilet facilities.
b. **Bustee dwellers** live in temporary homes made from cardboard, plastic sheeting, concrete pipes. Families sometimes share these huts.
c. Many people are homeless. Shortage of employment and very low wages force many (up to half a million) to live on the streets in Calcutta.

2. Shortage of Clean Water
a. Many people in Calcutta have no clean water. Many use unfiltered water for cooking and drinking. In some bustees, people must queue for long periods at water taps to await their turn.
b. Demand on city water supplies is great so the water systems are generally overworked.
c. Water in the Hooghly river, which flows through Calcutta, is sometimes salty due to sea water entering the river.

3. Pollution
a. Sewage facilities in Calcutta are inadequate. Many families often share a single toilet. Sewage and domestic waste regularly flow away through open drains in the bustees.
b. Garbage and litter pile up in the streets. At times these heaps become so large that volunteer groups remove them.
c. The overcrowded streets and temporary shacks cause noise and visual pollution.

4. Lack of Open Space
a. Because of the huge population almost every available patch of ground is occupied within the city.
b. Expanding shanty towns have spread far out into the countryside.

EFFECTS OF HIGH DENSITY POPULATION IN HONG KONG

1. Overcrowding
a. Schools operate a two-shift day in order to accommodate students.
b. Shanty town dwellers live in temporary homes made of poor building materials.
c. Many, especially refugees from Vietnam, live as 'boat people' in Hong Kong harbour.
d. Extended families live in overcrowded tenements with few services available.

2. Pollution
a. Large amounts of sewage and industrial waste are pumped into Hong Kong harbour each day.
b. Traffic congestion and car fumes pollute the air within the city.

3. Lack of Open Space
a. Ireland is 70 times larger than Hong Kong; yet Hong Kong has a population 1½ times that of Ireland.
b. Space is limited and most buildings are skyscrapers.
c. Hong Kong was overcrowded so new towns were built in the New Territories on the mainland.

EFFECTS OF LOW DENSITY POPULATION IN MALI

1. Low Marriage Rates
Young adults, especially males, leave rural areas for the cities. This reduces marriage opportunities in both areas as there is a surplus of males in the cities and a surplus of females in the rural areas.

2. Abandonment of Agricultural Land
a. Cities in countries such as Mali offer better health and educational facilities than rural areas. So many rural people abandon their land and move to the cities.
b. Drought and famine in parts of Mali have forced many herd owners to abandon their land. They move to cities such as Timbuktu in search of relief aid.

3. Political and Economic Isolation
a. During the nineteenth century, Mali became a French colony. As a result it was unable to develop independently and became politically weak and isolated.
b. Lack of roads and railways ensured that the country remained isolated. Much of Mali's mineral resources remain untouched as they are located in isolated places.

WHAT IS MEANT BY …
a. The North
The North represents the wealthy countries of the world e.g. Western Europe, North America, Japan and Australia.

b. The South
The South represents the poorest countries of the world e.g. India, most of Africa and South America. The South is often called the Third World.

FACTS ABOUT THE NORTH
1. Many countries of the North such as Spain, France and Britain were colonial powers. They once ruled countries of the South and used the resources of these countries to increase their own wealth.
2. Northern countries control world trade. Commodity prices such as sugar are set by Northern countries. This ensures that they remain wealthy.
3. Most people in Northern countries are healthy. High medical standards and a plentiful food supply ensure a healthy population. People live to old age.
4. Most Northern peoples are well educated. Most people stay at school until they are in their teens.
5. Incomes in the North are generally many times higher than those of the South.
6. Few children in families in the North.

FACTS ABOUT THE SOUTH

1. Many countries of the South, e.g. Mali and Brazil, were colonies of Northern countries. They remained poor while their rulers grew rich.
2. Southern countries are given low prices for their exports by Northern countries. So they are unable to repay their debts and they remain poor.
3. Many people in Southern countries are unhealthy. Low medical standards, a shortage of food and unclean water supplies cause diseases such as cholera. Many people die young.
4. Most Southern peoples are uneducated. Many leave school at a very young age.
5. Incomes in the South are many times smaller than those in the North.
6. Many children die under the age of five years.

REASONS WHY SO MANY CHILDREN DIE IN THE SOUTH

1. Lack of a balanced diet causes malnutrition and undernourishment. Famines in regions such as the Sahel in Africa have caused the deaths of millions of children.
2. Diseases such as Aids, which can pass from parent to child, cause death and suffering to children.
3. Lack of toilet facilities and clean water supplies cause disease. Diarrhoea is a major killer disease in the South.
4. Poor medical facilities and shortage of vaccines lead to ill health and death.

WAYS TO REDUCE CHILD MORTALITY IN THE SOUTH

1. **Prevent dehydration.** Diarrhoea causes loss of body fluids. This can be prevented by cheap remedies such as dioralite. It is a mixture of sugar, salt and water in a particular ratio.
2. Provide a **clean water supply** to people to eliminate water-borne diseases.
3. **Vaccines** would eliminate many diseases such as measles.
4. **Breast feeding.** Third World mothers often mix powdered baby foods with unclean water in unsterilised containers. This leads to diarrhoea. This could be avoided if mothers breastfed their children.
5. **Literacy and health education.** Education programmes are needed to ensure that new and better methods are maintained.

MIGRATION

Definitions
Pull factors are features about a place that appear attractive to people who are moving their home.
Push factors are features about a place that force people to move their home.

REASONS WHY PEOPLE LEAVE THE WEST OF IRELAND FOR DUBLIN
1. Farms in the west of Ireland are small and unprofitable. People are leaving the land for jobs in the cities.
2. As young people leave the west, the services (e.g. schools, recreational centres and hospitals) close. The region becomes unattractive to live in so more people leave the area.
3. Industry is reluctant to set up in an area where the work-force is limited. So jobs are few and people leave to find employment elsewhere.
4. Standards of living are lower in the west than the east of Ireland. Young people leave the west for better lifestyles in the east.

EFFECTS OF MIGRATION ON THE WEST OF IRELAND
1. Many people between the ages of 18 and 30 migrate from the area, so marriage rates and birth rates are low.
2. Farms are left in the care of older people who often lack the energy to work them fully. Many farms become neglected or abandoned when the older people die.
3. Industry is reluctant to set up in an area of low population and out-migration as the labour force is limited.
4. Community services and facilities decline as the population falls. This in turn reduces the attractiveness of the area for the young people.

EFFECTS OF MIGRATION ON DUBLIN
1. The population of Dublin has increased. Large suburbs and dormitory towns such as Tallaght have developed around the city.
2. Young people from the west of Ireland help to develop the city's economy e.g. new skills, purchasing houses.
3. Overcrowding may result in parts of the city. Great demand for accommodation raises prices and this may lead to overcrowding within the city.
4. Resources such as water supply, jobs and other services may be unable to cope with the demand, and overpopulation results.

REASONS WHY IRISH PEOPLE MIGRATED TO BRITAIN AND THE USA

Push Factors

1. The Famine (1845–49). The poverty of the west of Ireland after the Famine forced people to leave the region and seek a living elsewhere.
2. Repeal of the Corn Laws. Irish farmers changed over to dairy farming and cattle rearing. Thousands of farm labourers were unemployed and were forced to leave the country in search of work.
3. As young people left the west the services such as schools, recreational centres and hospitals closed. The region became unattractive to live in.
4. During the 1980s Ireland had a huge unemployment problem. People, especially young adults, were forced to leave the country in search of employment.

Pull Factors

Past Attractive Factors

1. The prospect of employment on the roads and railways, in construction and the police force encouraged people to move to Britain and the USA.
2. The prospect of land in America offered great opportunities to farmers' sons who would not inherit their parents' land.
3. The prospect of adventure and freedom in a new country was very attractive to young adults.

Recent Changing Migration Patterns in Ireland

1. The Celtic Tiger economy has increased the number and quality of jobs available in Ireland.
2. A well-educated work-force provides a rapidly growing economy with skilled labour.
3. Many foreign nationals come to Ireland to fill employment needs here. So now Ireland is a region of in-migration.

ORGANISED MIGRATION

CASE STUDY: THE PLANTATION OF ULSTER

Pull Factors
1. Planters were attracted to Ulster by promises of large estates at low cost. Estates were between 1000 and 2000 acres.
2. Scottish farmers were offered land from the landlords' estates at a low rent.
3. Religious groups were attracted to Ireland in order to establish the Protestant religion and English and Scottish cultures in Ulster.

Push Factors
1. Many Irish farmers were forced off their lands and fled to the forests.
2. Some Irish were moved to smaller estates in different parts of Ulster.
3. Some Irish chieftains were forced to flee the country and live in exile.

EFFECTS OF THE ULSTER PLANTATIONS
1. **Culture.** English and Scottish cultures, including the English language, were established in Ulster.
2. **Religious division.** Division between the Protestant planters and the Catholic Irish was a consequence of the plantation. This division may be partly to blame for the unrest in Northern Ireland.
3. **Towns.** Planned towns with a central square called a diamond were built in Ulster. Prior to the plantations there were no towns in Ulster as it was ruled by Gaelic chieftains.

CASE STUDY: EUROPEAN COLONISATION OF SOUTH AMERICA

Pull Factors
1. **Conquistadores.** Military men came to South America to conquer, and in search of gold. Huge fortunes in gold **(El Dorado)** were expected to be gained.
2. **Religion.** Missionaries came to convert the 'pagan' natives to Christianity.
3. **Planters.** Planters came in search of land. They created huge estates and kept the profits for themselves.
4. **Monarchs.** Monarchs, such as the king and queen of Spain, sponsored voyages of discovery to increase their wealth and influence in other parts of the world.

EFFECTS OF COLONISATION IN SOUTH AMERICA
1. Local Indian tribes were either killed or forced to work for the new planters.
2. Cultures such as the Inca culture were destroyed and replaced with Spanish culture and architectural styles.
3. Black African slaves were brought to South America where their descendants live today.
4. Towns and cities were established along the coasts of South America e.g. Rio de Janeiro and Lima.

CHAPTER 8   SETTLEMENTS

LOCATIONS OF IRISH SETTLEMENTS

EARLY IRISH SETTLEMENTS WERE LOCATED IN THE FOLLOWING PLACES:

1. On the northeast and east coasts because the earliest settlers had crossed over on land bridges from Britain.
2. On river banks, coastal estuaries and near lakes as they needed a fresh water and food supply.
3. Near rich farmland for rearing cattle and on upland where soils were light and easily tilled.
4. On elevated sites such as islands, cliffs and hill tops for safety from attack.

PATTERNS OF IRISH TOWNS

1. When towns are dotted evenly over an area they form a **scattered pattern** e.g. planned towns such as the towns in Ulster.
2. When towns occur in a line they form a **linear pattern** e.g. Viking towns along the east coast and towns along national primary routes leading to Dublin.
3. When towns occur together in a group they form a **clustered pattern** e.g. Malahide, Tallaght and Dublin.

WHY IRISH SETTLEMENTS AVOID HIGHLANDS

1. Many Irish highland areas are cold, wet and windy.
2. Many highland areas are steep-sided and so are difficult to build upon.
3. Routeways avoid highland areas so access is limited.

WHY IRISH SETTLEMENTS PREFER LOWLAND AREAS

1. Living conditions are generally warmer, drier and calmer than on highlands.
2. Flat or gentle slopes are easier to construct buildings on.
3. There is a denser network of routeways in lowland areas for easy access.
4. Market towns tend to develop in the centre of fertile plains.

IRISH TOWNS ARE LOCATED IN THE FOLLOWING PLACES:

1. On river banks for a fresh water supply.
2. At lowest bridging points near the sea where coastal routes meet e.g. Limerick city.
3. On raised sites (dry point sites) to avoid wet lowland areas e.g. Corrofin, Co. Clare.
4. In the centre of well-drained, fertile plains where routes meet e.g. Athlone, Co. Westmeath.
5. Near large estates where local landlords established towns e.g. Maynooth, Co. Kildare.

SETTLEMENT PATTERNS ON THE DUTCH POLDERS

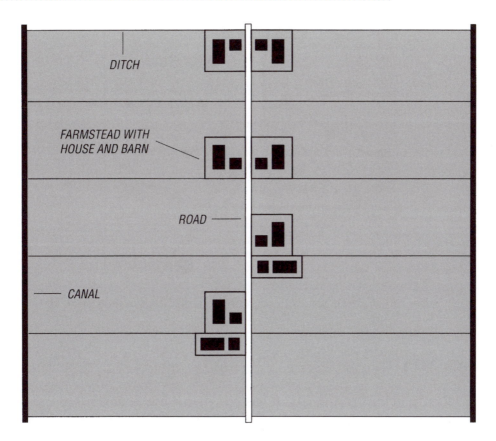

Fig 8.1 Linear settlement on the polders

1. FARMS AND FARMHOUSES

Farms and farmhouses are sited in a linear pattern along roads. Each farm has one side bordering a canal and one side bordering a road.

2. TOWNS AND VILLAGES

a. Towns are centrally placed and are foci of routeways. Each town provides the inhabitants of the surrounding villages and farms with goods and services.
b. Villages are planned in circles around new towns. They are connected to each other by a ring road and to Emmeloord by a series of radial roads.

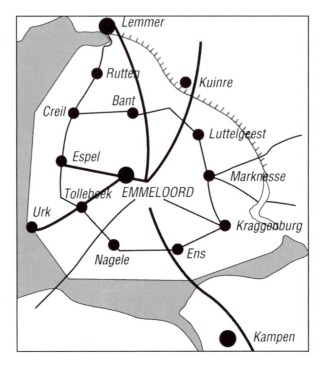

Fig 8.2 Planned villages around a central town, Emmeloord, on the polders

THE RANDSTAD

The word Randstad means **ring city**. It has grown in a **horseshoe** or semicircular **shape**. The Randstad is a horseshoe-shaped conurbation formed by the cities of The Hague, Amsterdam, Utrecht and Rotterdam.

GREENHEART

The greenheart is located at the centre of the Randstad. It is a pleasant, semi-rural area of farmland, parks and small towns and villages.

PROBLEM OF THE RANDSTAD

To protect the **greenheart** (farmland which still separates these cities) from being absorbed into the urban area.

Methods Used by the Planners
1. Placed strict controls on further building within the greenheart.
2. Directed people away from the Randstad into **overspill towns**.

CASE STUDY: ALMERE, AN OVERSPILL TOWN

WHY THE PLANNERS HAVE DEVELOPED ALMERE

1. To create an administrative centre for the southern Flevoland Polder.
2. To accommodate overspill population from Amsterdam.
3. To provide jobs and reduce commuting (daily movement) to and from Amsterdam.
4. To reduce the demand for building land within the Randstad.
5. To provide recreational facilities for the polders and Amsterdam.
6. To provide a good environment for the inhabitants of Almere.

FUNCTIONS OF NUCLEATED SETTLEMENTS

Definitions

The **functions** of a settlement are the services which it provides for its people and for the people of its surrounding area or hinterland.

A **settlement** is often classified according to its main function.

Most settlements are **multifunctional** — they perform several functions.

CLASSIFICATION OF SETTLEMENT BY FUNCTION

Village
A limited range of services for the surrounding rural area. Post office, shops.

Market Town
A marketing centre for sale of animals, vegetables; shops such as supermarkets and clothing; specialist services such as dentist; industries such as food processing.

> Examples: Limerick; Sligo

Defence Town
To protect inhabitants from attack; to control captured lands; to guard important sites.

> Examples: Athlone, Co. Westmeath; Limerick

Resource-Based Settlement
Mining town.

> Examples: Navan, Co. Meath

Residential/Dormitory Town
Towns in which people live and from which they commute each day to work.

> Examples: Malahide, Co. Dublin; Shannon New Town, Co. Clare

Recreational Towns
Spa resorts e.g. Lisdoonvarna in Co. Clare; coastal/seaside towns e.g. Tramore in Co. Waterford, Bray in Co. Wicklow.

Religious Towns
Centres of pilgrimage e.g. Knock in Co. Mayo. Seats of bishops e.g. Galway. Sites of abbeys and monasteries e.g. Ennis in Co. Clare.

CASE STUDY: LIMERICK IN THE SHANNON BASIN

REASONS WHY LIMERICK IS AN IMPORTANT PORT

1. It is located on the wide, deep and sheltered estuary of the River Shannon.
2. Its proximity to the continent of Europe facilitates the importing and exporting of goods.
3. There are many large heavy industries on its estuary e.g. Aughinish Alumina, Moneypoint Power Station.

REASONS WHY LIMERICK IS AN IMPORTANT MARKET CENTRE

1. It is centrally located in the fertile flood plain of the River Shannon.
2. It is near the Golden Vale, famous for its dairy farming.
3. It is on the lowest bridging point of the Shannon and is therefore the focus for many routes.
4. It was a major food processing centre up to about 1970.

REASONS WHY LIMERICK IS AN IMPORTANT RELIGIOUS CENTRE

1. Churches were built in Limerick as early as Norman times e.g. St Mary's Cathedral.
2. Limerick is the administration centre and the seat of a few bishops for a number of dioceses.
3. There are 18 churches in Limerick city offering services for many denominations.

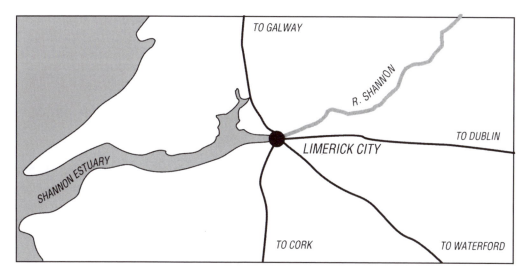

Fig 8.3 Limerick in the Shannon Basin

Settlements

CASE STUDY: COLOGNE IN THE RHINE BASIN

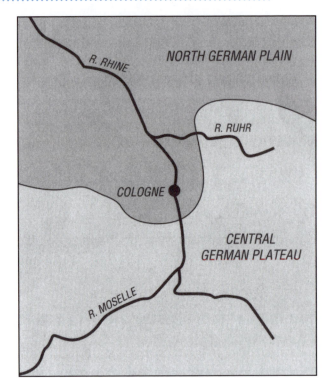

Fig 8.4 Cologne in the Rhine Basin

REASONS WHY COLOGNE IS AN IMPORTANT PORT
1. It is located on the wide and deep River Rhine.
2. It has a sheltered inland location.
3. It is situated at the meeting point of canal and River Rhine traffic.
4. It is an outlet for the exports of a large agricultural hinterland.
5. It is a manufacturing centre with many products for export e.g. iron and steel.

REASONS WHY COLOGNE IS AN IMPORTANT MARKET CENTRE
1. It is near the fertile lowland region of the North German Plain.
2. It is situated in the fertile flood plain of the Rhine.
3. It is located at the focus of routes for the surrounding region and at a crossing point of the Rhine.
4. It has numerous food processing industries e.g. flour milling.

REASONS WHY COLOGNE IS AN IMPORTANT RELIGIOUS CENTRE

1. It was a major centre of pilgrimage during the Middle Ages.
2. Four religious orders and an associated university were already in the city in 1388.
3. It is the administrative centre of the wealthiest arch-diocese in West Germany.

FUNCTIONS CHANGE OVER TIME

A MINING TOWN

CASE STUDY: NAVAN IN CO. MEATH

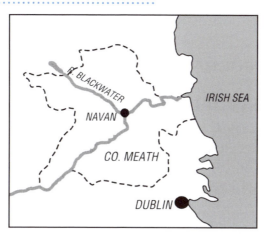

Fig 8.5 Navan in Co. Meath

FIRST FUNCTIONS OF NAVAN

1. Started as a religious centre.
2. It was a defence town during Norman times.
3. Then it prospered as a market town.
4. Today it is a mining town.

FUNCTIONS OF NAVAN AS A MINING TOWN

Navan provides:
1. a large, skilled work-force for Tara Mines;
2. a rail link to Dublin port for the export of ore;
3. housing, educational, commercial and other facilities for those people working for Tara Mines.

HOW NAVAN BENEFITS FROM TARA MINES

Tara Mines provide:
1. 700 jobs;
2. a higher standard of living;
3. €36m earned by local workers;
4. 'spin off' businesses for other economic activities such as construction and light engineering.

A MANUFACTURING CENTRE

Notice: Choose A, B or C for study

A. CASE STUDY: DROGHEDA

FIRST FUNCTIONS OF DROGHEDA

1. Built by the Vikings, Drogheda was first a port.
2. It became a defence town during Norman times.
3. During the fifteenth century the Irish Parliament met on occasions in Drogheda.
4. Today it is a manufacturing centre and port.

REASONS WHY DROGHEDA HAS ATTRACTED MANUFACTURING INDUSTRY

1. It is located on the east coast and has long-established trading links with England, Scotland, France and Spain.
2. It has a deep and sheltered harbour on the estuary of the Boyne.
3. It is a major bridging point of the Boyne river and a route focus in the area.
4. It has a rich hinterland, the basin of the Boyne; so it has attracted food processing industries.

SETTLEMENTS

OR

B. CASE STUDY: CLARECASTLE, CO. CLARE

FIRST FUNCTIONS OF CLARECASTLE

1. It developed as a crossing point/fording point on the River Fergus.
2. It became a defensive settlement when the Normans built a castle near the bridge. Later a military barracks was built by the British army.
3. It was an outport for Ennis, exporting grain to Britain.
4. In the 1970s a large chemical company built a factory near the village. Today it is a major manufacturing centre for this chemical company.

WHY IT ATTRACTED MANUFACTURING INDUSTRY

1. It had level land close to a major river, the Fergus.
2. It was near Ennis, a large town with an educated and skilled workforce.
3. It was close to Shannon International Airport for easy access and transport of goods.

OR

C. CASE STUDY YOUGHAL, CO. CORK

FIRST FUNCTIONS OF YOUGHAL

1. It was established as a trading centre by the Vikings.
2. Then it became a defence town during Norman times. This function lasted until the end of British rule in Ireland.
3. During the seventeenth century it was a major port. This function continues but it is now only a very small port.
4. During the nineteenth and twentieth centuries it was an important seaside resort.

RECENT FUNCTION

Since the 1980s Youghal has become an important manufacturing centre. Many companies have factories near the town producing surgical goods, textiles and DVDs.

MOVEMENT, COMMUNICATIONS LINKS AND THE DEVELOPMENT OF SETTLEMENTS

HOW THE IRISH ROAD NETWORK DEVELOPED

1. The regular movement of goods between inland towns and the coast led to the development of our roads.
2. Our present road network was begun in the eighteenth century.
3. Recently Irish roads have been straightened and widened.
4. Ring roads, by-passes, dual carriageways and motorways have all been built. The M50 motorway around Dublin has been completed.

The Development of Roads has Aided the Growth of Many Irish Towns

Bridging towns

Main roads converge (meet) at important bridging points on a river, such as the lowest bridging points along coastal estuaries. Defensive and important port settlements developed at such places.

Tourist towns

Modern road improvements have helped the development of tourism and so have helped tourist towns, such as Killarney and Galway, to prosper.

Dormitory towns

Modern routeways such as dual carriageways and motorways have helped the easy movement of commuters. This has led to the growth of dormitory and satellite towns near large cities such as Dublin.

Ordinary Course: Choose any one from A, B, C, D

Higher Course: Choose any two from A, B, C, D

A. EUROPEAN UNION (EU) AIRPORTS

Within the EU, air routes have focused on the following places:
1. Capital cities such as London and Paris;
2. Important industrial and commercial centres, such as Dusseldorf and Frankfurt;
3. Recreational and religious centres such as Alicante and Lourdes.

Why Air Transport has Grown in Recent Decades

1. Air travel has reduced travelling time.
2. Western European countries have become wealthier, so more people can now afford air travel.
3. Competition among airlines has brought about cheaper fares.
4. A greater number of flights are now available to a wider variety of places.

The Presence of Airports has Meant the Growth of Settlements

1. Tourism has led to the growth of numerous towns and cities, such as those in the Alps and along the Mediterranean coast (e.g. Benidorm and Marbella).
2. New towns, such as Shannon New Town, have developed near airports.
3. Established towns have expanded due to the extra trade created by air transport.

CASE STUDY: ALICANTE AIRPORT

1. In the 1950s large numbers of tourists were attracted to Spain's Costa Blanca.
2. They were attracted by the hot, dry summers and long, sandy beaches.
3. A large airport was built at Alicante to cater for the increasing numbers.
4. The airport drew more people to the area.
5. This led to the rapid growth of towns such as Benidorm.

CASE STUDY: SHANNON AIRPORT

1. Shannon lies between North America and western Europe. These air routes are among the busiest in the world. So Shannon has become an important international airport.
2. Shannon has led to the growth of Limerick and to the creation of Shannon New Town.
3. Shannon New Town was built to accommodate people who wanted to work at the airport. Today it is a large residential and dormitory town.

B. CASE STUDY: THE RIVER RHINE

WHY THE RHINE IS CALLED THE LIFELINE OF EUROPE
1. It is a wide and deep river which is navigable for large vessels as far inland as Basle.
2. Level lowland allowed the Rhine to be easily joined by canal to other major rivers in Europe such as the Rhone and Danube.
3. It passes through many European countries and they use it to import and export products.
4. It passes through the Ruhr which is the largest industrial area in Europe.

HOW THE RHINE LED TO THE GROWTH OF CITIES
1. Canals, dock areas and flat lowland near the river led to the growth of industrial areas on the Rhine.
2. Large ports such as Duisburg and Europoort were developed and are now huge industrial and warehouse centres.
3. Canalside cities such as Dortmund have prospered as a result of barge traffic.
4. The Rhine is a major tourist centre offering trips along the gorge. These bring extra business to Rhineside cities and towns.

C. INTERSTATE ROADS IN THE USA

Why the Interstate Roads were Built
1. Great public demand for a better road system.
2. Military people wanted to be able to move troops and weapons quickly throughout the country in case of war.
3. Fuel prices were low and the motor car was in common use.

How Interstate Roads have Led to the Growth of Cities
1. Better interstate roads increased the flow of traffic along routes.
2. Numbers of vehicles became so great that flyovers and spaghetti junctions were built.
3. The presence of interstate roads has led to urban sprawl as people commute huge distances to work. Los Angeles is an agglomeration of numerous cities such as Hollywood and Long Beach.
4. Some cities have become the focus of interstate highways e.g. Chicago.

D. THE FRENCH RAIL SYSTEM

Why French Railways are so Important Today

1. During World War 2 the French rail system was badly damaged so a new system was developed after the war.
2. A new electric railway system (TGV) was built for passengers only.
3. Trains travel at speeds of over 200 km per hour.
4. For passengers, it is comfortable and faster than air for medium-length journeys.
5. It has reduced traffic congestion on roads.

How the Railway in France has Led to the Growth of Cities

1. High-speed underground railways link up all parts of Paris.
2. The Metro and RER service a large area e.g. the airports and five new towns around Paris.
3. This service allows people to live outside the city and commute to work. So urban sprawl continues to grow.
4. The TGV has brought increased traffic to the cities of France such as Lille, Lyon and Marseille, and so has led to their growth.

THE DEVELOPMENT OF DUBLIN

STAGE 1 — VIKING DUBLIN

About A.D. 841 the Vikings established a settlement near a black pool (**Dubh Linn**) on the River Liffey. The Vikings were seafarers and traders and so Dublin developed as a port.

STAGE 2 — NORMAN DUBLIN

The Normans conquered Dublin in 1170. Dublin soon developed trading links with English towns. Dublin Castle was built in 1220 and so Dublin became a defensive town and administrative centre for all Ireland. Dublin expanded into a large city.

STAGE 3 — GEORGIAN DUBLIN

Most of Dublin as we know it today was built during the Georgian period (1714–1830).

Reasons Why This Occurred
1. Dublin was the seat of government so wealthy MPs built their mansions in the city.
2. Dublin's port was enlarged. The North Wall and South Wall were built to make it a sheltered harbour.
3. The Royal and Grand Canals were built which increased trade between Dublin and the midland towns.
4. Industries such as brewing thrived in the city.

STAGE 4 — NINETEENTH-CENTURY DUBLIN
The size and population of Dublin grew during the 1800s.

Reasons for this Growth
1. A rapid population growth and the effects of the Famine caused huge numbers of rural people to migrate to Dublin. They crowded into slums in the inner city.
2. The coming of the railway allowed people to live in nearby seaside towns such as Dun Laoghaire.
3. In 1800 the Act of Union abolished the Irish Parliament so MPs left central Dublin for the newly built suburbs.

STAGE 5 — THE PRESENT
Dublin has grown most rapidly during the twentieth and twenty-first centuries.

Reasons for this Growth
1. Dublin is Ireland's capital city. Company headquarters, the civil service and the Dáil are all based in Dublin.
2. Dublin is Ireland's main industrial centre. Companies such as Guinness, as well as modern industrial estates, offer a wide range of industrial jobs.
3. Dublin is Ireland's main port. Goods are imported and exported to other EU countries through Dublin port.
4. Dublin is Ireland's main educational centre. Colleges and universities such as Trinity College and University College Dublin are located in the city.
5. Dublin is a centre of in-migration. Over the past decades, thousands of people from rural Ireland have migrated to Dublin in search of employment.
6. A cluster of dormitory towns has developed around Dublin. Towns such as Malahide are inhabited by commuters i.e. people who work in the city and travel to work each day.

Settlements

FUNCTIONAL ZONES WITHIN NEW YORK CITY

CASE STUDY: MANHATTAN ISLAND IN NEW YORK CITY

BUSINESS
Wall Street with its stock exchange;
The Chrysler Building with its many offices.

SHOPPING
Fifth Avenue with shops such as Macy's;
Broadway for theatre and cinema.
Manhattan has many other shopping areas: Chinatown, an important area of oriental shopping; Radio City, an area of numerous different shops.

RESIDENTIAL
Harlem is a residential area where many black people live. It has become an area of increasing prosperity in recent years.

INDUSTRY
The southern tip of Manhattan has docks. But due to the need for fast transport and large storage areas the new docks are across the Hudson River in New Jersey.

RECREATION
Central Park is a huge rectangular area for recreation in the centre of Manhattan. Ice-skating in winter, pony rides, jogging and walking are some of the activities that occur in the park. Channel Promenade, with its ice rink and cafe, is a major focus for people in New York.

FUNCTIONAL ZONES WITHIN IRISH CITIES

1. LAND VALUE

The value of land increases towards the city centre. This is the busiest part of the city and so there is a great demand for city-centre land. People are willing to pay high prices for it e.g. on O'Connell Street, Grafton Street and Henry Street.

2. BUILDING HEIGHT

Because the price of land is high at the city centre, owners must make the best use of the available space. So they build high buildings. Many floors increase the ground space. Sky-scrapers and tall office blocks are located here e.g. Liberty Hall.

3. CITY HOUSING

a. Many dwellings in the inner city are often in need of repair. Many are rented and are left to deteriorate and fall into decay. When conditions force tenants to leave, these buildings are knocked down and replaced by office blocks and luxury apartments.

b. Housing is old and multi-storeyed at the city centre. As one approaches the suburbs, buildings get lower (two-storey and bungalow) and newer. Dwellings at the city centre are terraced; buildings in the suburbs are detached and semi-detached.

4. TRANSPORT

Each day there are two peak times in the movement of people:
1. **Morning rush hour**. People travel to work each morning between 7.30 am and 9.30 am.
2. **Evening rush hour**. People travel home each evening between 4.30 pm and 6.30 pm.

This pattern of movement causes traffic jams along routes.

Some Ways to Reduce Traffic Congestion
1. The introduction of roundabouts to speed up the flow of traffic.
2. The use of one-way traffic within the city centre to avoid traffic jams.
3. The use of bus lanes to speed up public transport.
4. Build motorways through cities and ring roads around cities to carry heavy traffic.
5. The use of electric railways, such as the Dart, in suburbs to limit cars within the city.
6. Building more multi-storey car parks to reduce street congestion.

URBAN PROBLEMS

INNER CITY DECAY

1. Many dwellings in the inner city are old and in need of repair. Many have inadequate or no indoor bathrooms or toilets. Many dwellings are divided into flats and are generally overcrowded.
2. Undeveloped sites are used as rubbish dumps and graffiti stains surrounding walls, creating visual pollution.
3. Young people leave inner city areas for new housing estates in the suburbs. An aging population remains in the city.
4. As young people leave the inner city, services such as schools and community halls close. This encourages more young people to leave the area.

INADEQUATE SERVICES

1. As previously mentioned, when young people leave the inner city, services such as schools and community halls close.
2. Streets are congested with traffic. Due to the increased use of cars, old and narrow streets of the inner city areas are unable to cope with such traffic.
3. Housing is old and inadequate.

COMMUNITY DISRUPTION

1. Close community ties are broken when people move from the inner city to the suburbs. In the inner city, relations (e.g. brothers and sisters) live near each other, often in the same flat complex. This is no longer possible when some move to the suburbs.
2. High-cost office blocks regularly replace inner city housing in redevelopment plans. Communities are not allowed to rebuild in the same spot. So they are moved to the suburbs where families and friends are housed far apart from each other.

UNEMPLOYMENT

1. Due to lack of space and transport access, many inner city industries have closed and moved to the suburbs.
2. Lack of a proper education due to poverty regularly leads to unemployment within the inner city communities.
3. Lower-income suburbs often have high unemployment rates.

CRIME

Some places in Irish cities are classed as 'no go' areas. These are often the poorest parts of the cities. Poor housing, lack of education and recreation facilities and unemployment all lead to crime.

URBAN SPRAWL

Urban sprawl is the rapid spread of housing from cities out into the countryside.
1. Valuable farmland and green belts are taken over by roads and buildings.
2. Villages near to cities are swallowed up. They themselves grow into huge towns such as Tallaght and Malahide.
3. The ever-growing suburbs increase the demand for services e.g. sewage, telecommunications, water supply. This demand increases taxes.

SOLUTIONS TO SOME URBAN PROBLEMS

SOLUTIONS TO INNER CITY DECAY

1. Special designated areas within parts of the inner city are zoned for redevelopment. Tax benefits and rates reductions are given to owners and occupiers of redeveloped properties.
2. Repairs to old dwellings and the building of new ones improves the appearance of inner city areas.
3. Derelict sites should be redeveloped for the building of houses or apartments.
4. Zones of light industry should be available to inner city areas to encourage young people to stay in the area.
5. The visual as well as the structural environment of inner city areas should be upgraded. For instance, tree planting along pavements, repaired and improved pavements, the erection of traditional shop fronts; all these add to the character of inner city areas.

SOLUTION TO OVERCROWDING IN THE CITIES

New towns are built to cater for the overspill populations of large cities e.g. Tallaght and Shannon New Town.

They have the following advantages for people:
1. They are specially designed to cater for large populations.
2. They contain new housing estates with specially designed shopping centres.
3. They contain planned industrial estates to cater for a large work-force.
4. They are near large cities for specialist services.

CHAPTER 9   NATURAL RESOURCES

OIL EXPLORATION

Definitions

Finite resource. Non-renewable fuels such as oil, coal, natural gas and peat will no longer be available to people when their supplies are burned. Once it is burned it cannot be used again.

Infinite resource. Renewable resources such as wind, waves and falling water can be used again and again.

LARGE QUANTITIES OF ENERGY ARE USED BY SOCIETY TODAY IN THE FOLLOWING WAYS:

1. Domestic activities; televisions, heaters, cookers, lights (35%).
2. Manufacturing; machines, lighting, welding, heating (30%).
3. Transport; fuels for cars, buses, tractors, aeroplanes (20%).
4. Commercial; shop lighting, heating, signs (15%).

ADVANTAGES OF OIL AS A FUEL

1. It is cheap, plentiful and easy to handle and transport.
2. It is a clean fuel to burn, giving off little smoke or fumes.
3. It is an efficient fuel giving off great heat.

OIL EXPLORATION IN THE CELTIC SEA

SEARCHING FOR OIL

1. The Celtic Sea is divided into blocks on a map. Oil companies rent these rectangular sea areas.
2. An option is taken on individual blocks so that companies can carry out rock tests to check for the presence of oil or gas.
3. If rock formations look promising, companies may drill test holes.
4. If sufficient supplies of oil or gas are found then they will bring the supplies ashore.

Present Supplies
a. Gas has been discovered and exploited off the Old Head of Kinsale.
b. New gas deposits have been found off the coast of Co. Mayo. This area is called the Corrib field.

ADVANTAGES OF THE CELTIC SEA FOR EXPLORATION OF OIL OR GAS
1. The continental shelf stretches for over 200 km off the south Irish coast. The shallow waters make the exploitation of the supplies easy to control and cheap to produce.
2. The sheltered harbours of the south coast offer excellent facilities for backup industries servicing the rigs.
3. An oil refinery is already located in Cork harbour which would refine oil if it were discovered.
4. The Celtic Sea is near to EU markets where there is a large demand for oil.

EFFECTS OF LARGE-SCALE OIL DEPOSITS IN THE CELTIC SEA
Positive Effects
1. New industries would be set up to service the oil rigs e.g. catering.
2. The manufacture of rigs and construction of houses would lead to more jobs.
3. Roads, ports and other services would be upgraded.
4. New oil-based industries would create extra employment.

Negative Effects
1. Increases in the demand for houses would raise prices for locals.
2. Oil spills would cause great damage to wildlife and beaches.
3. Oil rigs and the increase in heavy engineering in the area would lead to visual pollution.

HIGHER COURSE ONLY

OIL EXPLORATION IN SAUDI ARABIA

OPEC is the Organisation of Petroleum and Exporting Countries. Saudi Arabia is a member of OPEC.

OPEC controls oil prices in Arab countries.

DEVELOPMENT OF SAUDI OIL

1. Oil was first produced in Saudi Arabia by European and American oil companies. Most of the profits went to these companies; little went to Saudi Arabia.
2. With the establishment of OPEC in the 1960s Saudi Arabia forced oil companies to pay proper market prices for their oil.
3. This price rise caused an oil crisis in Europe and Ireland so encouraging them to search for oil in their own areas such as the Celtic Sea.

HOW OIL HAS BENEFITED SAUDI ARABIA

1. Saudi Arabia is one of the richest countries in the world due to oil earnings.
2. Many modern cities, hospitals and schools have been built which have raised the standard of living for its people.
3. All Saudi people are gainfully employed.
4. Many foreign skilled people are employed in Saudi Arabia. They pass on their skills to native people.

WOMEN IN SAUDI ARABIA

Little has changed for women in Saudi Arabia. Women are forbidden many things e.g. to drive cars and to work outside the home.

Some have been able to break away from this tradition. Education has helped some women to develop their own careers.

PEAT PRODUCTION IN THE MIDLANDS

IN THE PAST BOGS WERE DIFFICULT TO DEVELOP BECAUSE:
1. They were saturated with water and it was difficult to drag bundles of turf over spongy ground.
2. Turf was cut by hand using a **slean**. Only small amounts could be cut in a day.
3. Movement of turf from the midlands or mountains to people's homes was difficult as transport was slow.

TODAY BOGS ARE EASY TO DEVELOP BECAUSE:
1. Bord na Móna, a semi-state company, was set up specially to develop the bogs.
2. Large track machines are used to strip, level and drain the bogs.
3. Specially-designed machines such as **baggers** are used to cut enormous amounts of peat sods in a day.
4. Special machines such as a **milling machine**, **spoon harrow** and **ridger** are used to harvest milled peat.
5. Electricity-generating stations were designed to use peat as a fuel e.g. Allenwood and Littleton.
6. Railway lines were laid on bog surfaces to transport peat to the generating stations and to roadside depots.

PEAT PRODUCTS PRODUCED BY BORD NA MÓNA
1. **Sod turf** used in solid fuel cookers and open fires.
2. **Milled peat** used in power stations and in the manufacture of briquettes.
3. **Moss peat** used in gardening and as bedding for poultry.

Harvesting Methods
Sod peat
Turf sods are spread out on the surface of the bog to dry in the sun.

Milled peat
The top centimetre of the bog is rotavated into powder form, spread out on the bog surface and dried by the sun and breeze. It is then collected into long ridges and covered with plastic.

Moss peat

The bog surface is powdered down to a fine till which is then cleaned and packed in plastic.

TYPE OF BOGS

1. **Raised bogs** are deep (8 metres). They are located in the central plain.
2. **Blanket bogs** are shallow (1–2 metres). They are located on the mountains throughout Ireland.

ADVANTAGES OF DEVELOPING OUR BOGS

1. Bord na Móna creates employment and helps to reduce emigration.
2. Uses native fuel for industrial and domestic heating.
3. It reduces our imports of coal and oil.
4. ESB uses peat to generate electricity.
5. Export of peat products brings foreign money into Ireland.

OVER-EXPLOITATION OF A RESOURCE IN THE CELTIC SEA

THERE ARE THREE MAIN TYPES OF FISH IN IRISH WATERS

1. **Pelagic** fish e.g. herring or salmon.
   Pelagic fish swim near the surface. They are caught by drift net or ring net.
2. **Demersal** fish e.g. cod.
   Demersal fish are found near to the sea bed. They are caught by trawling.
3. **Shellfish** e.g. lobster.
   Some shellfish are caught on the sea bed in pots e.g. lobster pots.

Overfishing generally occurs in continental shelf areas which are rich in **plankton**. For example:

1. N.E. Atlantic along the coast of western Europe and Ireland,
2. N.W. Atlantic near Newfoundland,
3. N.E. Pacific near Alaska and California,
4. N.W. Pacific near China,
5. S.E. Pacific near Peru.

NATURAL RESOURCES

REASONS WHY IRISH WATERS ARE EXCELLENT FISHING AREAS

1. Ireland is situated on the continental shelf. These shallow waters contain vast amounts of plankton which fish eat.
2. The warm North Atlantic Drift brings extra supplies of fish food to Irish waters. Its warm waters also bring many varieties of fish.
3. Fish types generally occur in large shoals and are easy to catch.
4. Fish such as herring, mackerel and salmon are good to eat and they have a high commercial value.
5. The bays of western and southern Ireland provide sheltered harbours for fishing fleets.
6. Irish waters are relatively free from industrial waste making them a desirable source of fish.

Notice: Choose A or B for study

A REASONS FOR OVERFISHING IN THE CELTIC SEA

CASE STUDY: HERRING

1. Herring follow definite predictable movements before spawning. They move slowly, in huge numbers and to the same places each year to spawn. This makes them easy to catch.
2. The spawning grounds are in sheltered, shallow waters near the south Irish coast which can be fished even in stormy weather.
3. Herring are in their best condition just before spawning and so they fetch high prices.

WAYS TO PREVENT OVERFISHING IN THE CELTIC SEA

1. The EU sets **quotas** which limit the amounts of fish each member state may catch each year.
2. Only Irish trawlers may fish within 10 km of the Irish coast.
3. Only EU trawlers may fish within 20 km of the Irish coast.
4. Net mesh sizes are controlled to allow small fish to pass through without harm.
5. Surveys are constantly done to ensure that fish stocks are okay.

OR

B. REASONS FOR OVERFISHING IN IRISH WATERS

CASE STUDY: SALMON FISHING

1. Salmon follow definite predictable movements before spawning. They follow the coastline close to the surface and towards river estuaries from which they came originally.
2. They are large fish whose flesh is much sought after and so they fetch high prices.
3. They are caught in early spring and throughout the summer. Fishing at sea is relatively safe at this time of year with long days to increase catches.
4. **Monofilament** nets of illegal length, depth and mesh size are used which are invisible to fish.

WAYS TO PREVENT OVERFISHING OF SALMON
1. Drift netting at sea is now illegal. Extra patrol vessels must be used to prevent illegal fishing.
2. All salmon sold must be recorded to prevent poaching and illegal netting.
3. Stiffer penalties for offenders must be introduced and enforced.
4. The cost of salmon should be reduced so as to make it unattractive for poachers to operate.

CHAPTER 10 ECONOMIC ACTIVITIES

Definitions

Primary Activity: This provides unprocessed raw materials from the earth's surface — from rocks, soils and waters. Examples — farming, fishing, forestry, mining.

Secondary Activity (Manufacturing): Factories use raw materials and process (change) them into other products. Examples — engineering, chemicals, iron and steel.

Tertiary Activity: This activity is one which provides a useful service or facility. Examples — teaching, hairdressing, nursing, truck driving.

FARMING — A PRIMARY ACTIVITY

FARMING ON A LOCAL MIXED FARM IN THE EAST OR SOUTH OF IRELAND — AN EXAMPLE OF A SYSTEM

A system uses **inputs** (raw materials), processes them or changes them into **outputs** (finished products).

FARM INPUTS

1. Climate (heat, sunshine, rainfall)
2. Land (soil, drainage)
3. Stock (animals, seed)
4. Farm buildings (barn, silage pit, grain silos)
5. Labour (farmer and farm workers)
6. Machinery (tractor, milking machine, plough)
7. Capital (money)
8. Fertiliser
9. Animal feed

FARM PROCESSES

a. Crop farming
   1. ploughing
   2. rotavating
   3. planting
   4. harvesting
b. dairy farming
   1. milking
   2. feeding
   3. breeding

FARM OUTPUTS

a. Crop farming
   1. grain
   2. vegetables
   3. straw

b. dairy farming
   1. milk
   2. calves
   3. fertiliser (manure)

FACTORS WHICH FAVOUR CROP FARMING (TILLAGE)

1. Deep, well-drained soils which are light and easy to till.
2. Gently-sloping land with large fields. This makes machines easy to use.
3. A dry and sunny climate. This aids the ripening and harvesting of grain.
4. Proximity to large urban centres for markets e.g. Guinness in Dublin and Midleton distilleries in Co. Cork.
5. Near food processing centres for frozen and tinned food products.

FACTORS WHICH FAVOUR DAIRY FARMING

1. Soft rain all year provides a good growth of rich grass especially in spring and summer.
2. Limestone soils produce grass rich in calcium. This is essential for bone and body building in animals and for milk with a high butter fat content.
3. Mild winters mean a short indoor feeding season.
4. Food processing co-operatives which provide a ready market for a farmer's produce.

Disadvantages of Farming to the Environment

1. Sprays and insecticides may add poisonous chemicals to the soil which could later end up in food.

Economic Activities

2. Fertilisers which are used for plant growth may be washed into rivers and lakes. They cause an increase in algae and plant growth in these waters. This reduces the oxygen supply for fish.
3. Hedges are cut down to make way for increased farmland, so birds' habitats are reduced.
4. Silage and slurry effluent as well as milk are dumped into streams and rivers. These cause **eutrophication** (no oxygen) and severe fish kills.

SECONDARY ACTIVITY

A factory uses inputs (raw materials), processes or changes them into outputs (finished products).

Some finished products can then be used as raw materials by other factories:
e.g. wheat → milled → flour
    flour → baked → bread

MANUFACTURING INDUSTRY

Definitions

Heavy industry. Processes heavy or bulky raw materials into finished products e.g. iron ore and coal are used in the manufacture of steel.

Light industry. Uses small or lightweight raw materials for processing into finished products e.g. the manufacture of computers.

Footloose industry. One which can locate in a wide variety of places as no single locational factor dominates the choice of site e.g. electronics.

Industrialised	Industrialised countries or regions are found in the North. They have well-established industries and a high proportion of their populations work in industry. Example: Germany.
Newly industrialised	Most of the newly industrialised regions or countries are found in the South. Industrial growth is rapid. A small proportion of their populations work in industry. Example: Brazil, India.
Industrially emergent	All these regions or countries are found in the South. They are not industrialised. Example: Peru.

FACTORS WHICH INFLUENCE THE LOCATION OF A FACTORY

1. Raw Materials
Factories locate close to the raw material source or near to a port or airport for easy import of goods.

2. Transport
Modern factories locate near to ports, airports or major roadways for the easy movement of raw materials and finished products.

3. Markets
Transport of the finished product is generally more expensive than transport of raw materials. So factories tend to locate as close to large cities and high density regions as is possible e.g. EU.

4. Labour Force
Factories locate near to towns and cities to avail of a well-educated and skilled labour force.

5. Government Policies
Governments and the EU have policies which offer grants and incentives to factories which locate in their areas. Ireland has specially designed industrial estates which cater for industry only.

6. Capital
Factories need money to set up. Banks and other financial institutions must loan money at attractive rates to encourage companies to set up a factory.

7. Personal Factors
People may set up factories in a certain place because they were born in that area: Fiacla Toothpaste set up in Bray because it was the home of the company's founder.

In the Past
Old industry was often tied to particular locations. For example:

1. Iron and steel were tied to coalfield sites as it was cheaper to transport the iron ore than to transport the coal.
2. Textiles were tied to riverside sites for the washing and dyeing of wool.

Today — Modern Industry

1. Iron and steel industries have located on coastal sites as oil and gas can be used as a source of energy.
2. Textiles are footloose as electricity and water are available throughout the country.

Notice: Higher Course only — Choose A or B for study

LIGHT INDUSTRY AS A SYSTEM

A. CASE STUDY: DELL IRELAND

Dell Ireland is Ireland's largest computer manufacturer.

Inputs
1. Large factory building
2. Skilled work-force
3. Computer parts
4. Packaging material
5. Capital

Processes
1. Assembling PC computers and notebooks
2. Designing new products
3. Monitoring air quality
4. Packaging computer products
5. Organising products for distribution

Outputs
PCs, notebooks, printers, projectors.

REASONS WHY DELL IS LOCATED IN LIMERICK (DELL IS A FOOTLOOSE INDUSTRY)

1. Limerick is near to Shannon Airport, for the import and export of goods and easy access for overseas personnel.
2. The University of Limerick is nearby for research and a skilled graduate work-force.

ECONOMIC ACTIVITIES

3. Raheen had a planned industrial estate which is fully serviced with fibre optic telephone lines, nearby courier services and a communications network.
4. Large IDA grants and access to EU, Middle East and African markets were available.
5. The industrial estate is located on a national primary road which allows for the easy movement of raw materials and finished products.

OR

B. CASE STUDY: PC PRO

Inputs
1. Large factory building
2. Skilled work-force
3. Capital
4. Computer parts
5. Packaging material

Processes
1. Assembling computer parts
2. Quality control – checking computers
3. Packaging computers
4. Loading and unloading trucks

Output
Computers, printers, notebooks.

REASONS WHY PC PRO LOCATED IN CORK
1. Southside Industrial Estate is located near Cork City where a skilled work-force was available.
2. Southside Industrial Estate was serviced with fibre optic telephone lines and specially equipped for industry.
3. A printing plant, packaging plant and courier services were available locally.
4. Near Cork airport and major roads for importing and exporting.

OR

ECONOMIC ACTIVITIES

C. CASE STUDY: INTEL IRELAND LTD

Inputs
1. Water — nine million litres per day
2. Silicon wafers
3. Fibres for electric circuits
4. Microtechnology facilities

Processes
1. Manufacturing microchips
2. Creating electric circuits
3. Quality control of microchips
4. Packaging microchips
5. Monitoring air quality

Outputs
Microchips

REASONS WHY INTEL IRELAND LTD LOCATED IN LEIXSLIP
1. Large numbers of educated engineering and science graduates available.
2. Ireland is ideal for companies that wish to access the EU market.
3. Telecommunications services and a large water supply are available locally.
4. Leixlip is close to Dublin, which is Ireland's largest city.
5. The bedrock of the region is very stable and free from vibrations.

HEAVY INDUSTRY AS A SYSTEM

Notice: Higher Course only — choose A, B or C

A. CASE STUDY: READYMIX OF NAAS

Readymix makes concrete products.

Inputs
1. Gravel
2. Rock aggregates
3. Water
4. Cement
5. Large loading machines
6. Crushers

Processes
1. Grading aggregates
2. Loading trucks
3. Making tiles, blocks, concrete pipes and concrete

Outputs
1. Concrete
2. Concrete tiles
3. Concrete blocks and pipes

WHY READYMIX LOCATED AT NAAS
1. A large supply of gravel and rock from local quarries is available.
2. Near to Dublin and other large towns where concrete products are in constant demand.
3. Located in a densely populated region where a plentiful labour supply is available.
4. Located near a major road network for distribution of products.

OR

B. CASE STUDY: AUGHINISH ALUMINA

Aughinish Alumina refines alumina for aluminium products.

Inputs
1. Bauxite is imported from the Republic of Guinea
2. A marine terminal for unloading the bauxite
3. A workforce of 700 people
4. Caustic soda
5. Fuel oil
6. Electricity

Processes
1. Bauxite is crushed to a powder
2. Bauxite is mixed with caustic soda and then heated
3. Impurities are extracted
4. Red mud waste is pumped into a settling pond

Outputs
1. Alumina powder
2. Red mud waste
3. Caustic soda is recycled

OR

C. CASE STUDY: MONEYPOINT POWER STATION

Moneypoint is located on the Shannon estuary.

Inputs
1. Coal
2. Furnaces
3. Storage yards for coal
4. Quayside for unloading ships
5. Turbines
6. Electricians
7. Generation station
8. Water

Processes
1. Generating energy
2. Creating heat in furnaces
3. Generating steam
4. Electric cables
5. Monitoring energy levels

Output
1. Energy
2. Fumes from chimney stacks
3. Coal ash

REASONS FOR LOCATION ON THE SHANNON
1. A deep estuary capable of accomodating large coal tankers.
2. A sheltered harbour for easy and safe unloading of ships.
3. Near a large water supply — the river (needed to generate steam).
4. A skilled labour force available locally.

Economic Activities

Notice: Higher Course only

INDUSTRIAL LOCATIONS — A CHANGE OVER TIME

CASE STUDY: THE BRITISH IRON AND STEEL INDUSTRY

CHANGING LOCATIONS IN BRITAIN'S IRON AND STEEL INDUSTRY

18th Century

Energy supply — water

Inputs	**Output**
Iron ore	iron
charcoal	

Factories were located near to

a. rocks containing iron ore
b. forests from which charcoal was made
c. rivers to turn water wheels for power
d. rivers and canals for transport.

19th Century

Energy supply — coal

Inputs	**Outputs**
Iron ore	iron and steel
coal	

Factories were located near to

a. rocks containing iron ore
b. coalfields for coal
c. rivers, canals and railways for transport.

20th Century

Energy supply — coal, gas and oil, electricity

143

Economic Activities

Inputs   **Outputs**
Iron ore   iron and steel
coal, gas or oil

Factories were located near to
a. the coast for easy import or cheap iron ore from Sweden and Australia.
b. deep water bays to cater for large bulk carriers.

Other factors
c. oil and gas are cleaner, easy to handle and give off great heat.
d. local supplies of high-grade iron ore were exhausted.
e. plenty of flat land to lay out and build new factories.
f. scrap metal is easily imported.

Example of a coastal iron and steel plant: Port Talbot in Wales

Despite all of these changes, some iron and steel plants remained at their original locations. This is called **industrial inertia**.

CASE STUDY: SHEFFIELD STEEL

Industries remained here for the following reasons:
1. The tradition and reputation of steel making in the region helps sell Sheffield's products.
2. A skilled labour force is available in the area.
3. Grants are given by the British government to make the industry competitive with newer industrial plants along the coast. This prevents unemployment in the region.

WOMEN IN INDUSTRY
DEVELOPING COUNTRIES

In developing countries many women still work in the home.

Those Who Do Work in Industry
- work long hours
- receive little pay
- work in poor working conditions
- have no say in management

ECONOMIC ACTIVITIES

In developed countries many women work in industry.

Changes have Taken Place, such as
- many women are in paid employment
- many are employed in skilled and semi-skilled jobs
- women's wages have increased.

But in Ireland
- many women have only part-time jobs
- many continue to work in traditionally suitable jobs such as office work, cleaning, catering, factory operators
- these jobs are lower paid than male jobs (women earn only 75% of men's wages)
- few hold managerial positions e.g. in Ireland there are more female than male teachers. However, men occupy the majority of managerial positions.

Factors which Hinder Change
1. Some people still have set ideas about suitable jobs for women.
2. Irish schools cater for girls and boys in different ways such as choice of subjects. In school girls study home economics whereas boys study mechanical drawing.
3. Women are expected to do many of the domestic jobs in the home: cooking, ironing etc.

Notice: Higher Course only

WOMEN AT WORK

CASE STUDY: RUSSIA

In 1917 a people's revolution overthrew the Tzar, and Russia became the first communist country. As a result great social changes took place in Russia.

BEFORE THE REVOLUTION

- Women had few rights. They were expected to stay at home, rear families and obey their husbands.
- Most women could not read or write.
- Few worked in paid employment except in domestic duties.

AFTER THE REVOLUTION

- Men and women had equal rights.
- Women and men received equal treatment.
- Most women are literate.
- Men and women receive equal pay for equal work.
- Many women work in paid employment.

REASONS WHY MORE WOMEN WORK OUTSIDE THE HOME

1. They feel more fulfilled in their daily life.
2. They are more independent as they have their own source of income.
3. Their family is financially better off with an extra income.
4. They meet more people which keeps them up to date with world affairs.
5. They gain a separate identity from their husbands.

EFFECTS OF INDUSTRY ON AGRICULTURE, FORESTRY, TOURISM AND THE ENVIRONMENT

Positive Effects on Agriculture

- Provides a guaranteed market for farm products (**co-operatives**).
- Raises the quality of farm produce by regular testing.
- Continuous research provides new products from raw materials.
- Raises farmers' living standards.

Negative Effects on Agriculture

- Toxic fumes may cause illness to farm animals. Plants may suffer from leaf damage and stunted growth.
- Much farmland is lost to development sites for industry.

Positive Effects on Forestry (Silviculture)

- Industry creates a demand for wood, so more and more trees are planted each year.
- Increased forests lead to the protection of wildlife such as birds and animals.
- Increased forests provide picnic areas and forest walks.

Negative Effects on Forestry

- Acid rain causes damage to trees such as needle loss, root damage, bark injuries. Trees often die.
- Rapid removal of forest cover causes soil erosion, flooding (Bangladesh), extinction of bird and animal species as well as unique indigenous cultures in the Amazon forest.

Positive Effects on Quality of Life

- Industrial wages are high providing a large disposable income.
- Shorter working hours increase leisure time.
- Industry creates employment which in turn provides a wide variety of skills.
- Industry often sponsors sporting and community functions as well as providing scholarships in many sciences.

Negative Effects on Quality of Life

- Air pollution causes the **Greenhouse Effect.**
- Toxic fumes increase health risks including asthma and bronchitis.
- Factory effluent causes fish kills and contamination of shellfish.

CHAPTER 11   ECONOMIC INEQUALITY

FACTORS WHICH SLOW ECONOMIC DEVELOPMENT

1. Colonialism
2. Spending on arms and war
3. Rapid population growth
4. Climatic change

1. COLONIALISM

Effects of Colonialism on Ireland

a. Land ownership. Irish land was transferred from Catholic to Protestant owners. In the 17th century many Catholic landowners were evicted from their property and were forced to settle on small poorer farms in Connaught.
b. The new landowners were **absentee landlords** and so profits were sent abroad. So money for the development of local industries was not available.
c. Laws were passed which forced Ireland to provide England with raw materials such as grain and meat. As a result large estates were created for the growing of food for export abroad.
d. During the Famine, Ireland exported large amounts of food. Because this food was not available to Irish people, over one million people died from starvation.
e. Industries which may have competed with English trade were not allowed to open.
f. Ireland exported raw materials at a low price while it imported finished products at a high price. So Irish people became poorer.

CASE STUDY: SUGAR

SUGAR AND COLONIALISM

a. Sugar was produced from sugar cane on plantations. The raw sugar was exported to Europe for refining and then sold. Sugar profits ended up in Europe.
b. Slaves were used to work on the plantations. These people came from West Africa and were transported to the Americas for sale to plantation owners.
c. Some regions produced only sugar and became dependent on this one crop.
d. Colonialism prevented sugar processing industries from setting up. This caused places such as the West Indies to remain poor and weak while European countries such as Britain became rich and powerful.
e. The sugar trade was a factor in the creation of the North/South divide that exists today. Countries of the South receive low prices for their raw materials. They pay high prices for their imports. So they have constant difficulties saving money to build up their transport, health and industrial facilities.

THE SUGAR CROP TODAY

a. Developed countries no longer depend on 'the sugar-producing' regions for their total supply. Sugar beet, which grows in temperate countries, supplies one third of world demand.
b. Sugar substitutes are used in some processed foods.
c. There is a world surplus of sugar. This has reduced the price of sugar in the producing regions, so lowering their incomes.
d. As the buying power of sugar-producing regions declines so does the amount of money for investment, services and imports. So a cycle of poverty begins.

2. SPENDING ON ARMS AND WAR
a. Money which should be spent on roads, health and educational facilities, and agriculture is diverted to military uses.
b. Damage to property, housing, telecommunications, food production and ports during civil war prevents a country developing.
c. Deaths, famine and disease as a result of war reduces a country's ability to recover even when peace returns.
d. Military rulers often take control of the governments of unstable nations. This may cause excess spending on arms and military equipment.

3. RAPID POPULATION GROWTH
a. High birth rates create a strain on resources. Increased food production is immediately used up by the increase in population.
b. Urban services such as sewerage, water supply and rubbish disposal are unable to cope with increasing demands.
c. The lack of a social welfare system for the elderly encourages parents to have large families. This in turn causes an economic burden on parents.

4. CLIMATIC CHANGE
a. In Africa the climate is getting drier especially in areas bordering the deserts. Farmland is being destroyed, animals die, crops wither. People's lives are at risk, they are undernourished and are unable to work.
b. Resources are used to cope with emergency aid and so funds for long-term development projects are limited.

SOME SOLUTIONS TO INEQUALITIES OF NORTH/SOUTH DIVIDE
1. Educate people in the developed countries about the real causes of world inequality.
2. Get the 'Super Powers' to reduce their manufacture and sale of arms. In this way developing countries may not be encouraged to spend money on destructive resources.
3. Fairer trading practices should be encouraged between North and South.
4. Interference in national policies in the South by developed countries should be restricted.

INTERNATIONAL AID TO THE SOUTH

TYPES OF AID

1. Non-Governmental Organisations (NGOs)
Voluntary organisations such as Trócaire, Concern and Gorta provide both **emergency aid** and **development aid**.

2. Bilateral
This is direct aid from one government to another. Generally this type of aid is used to improve agriculture, education, health services.

3. Multilateral
International institutions such as the Red Cross, the United Nations and the World Bank provide both emergency and development aid.

IRISH AID PROGRAMMES — BILATERAL AID

These include programmes in Zambia, Tanzania, Uganda, Ethiopia, Mozambique and Lesotho.

1. Sponsored Programmes in Zambia
a. **Irish aid** helped the School of Veterinary Medicine at the **University of Zambia** to **educate** more **veterinary surgeons.**
b. **Rural water supply projects** included the **construction** of wells in rural villages to improve water quality and health facilities.

2. Sponsored Programme in Lesotho
This programme helped lay gravel roads using local labour in remote regions. These regions now have better access to essential basic services.

ADVANTAGES OF INTERNATIONAL AID

1. During emergencies, international aid saves countless lives as it has the means to act immediately in any given situation.
2. Agricultural output, health and education facilities improve as a result of increased funding and expert advice.
3. Aid allows the poorer areas of the world to receive a more equitable amount of the earth's resources such as money, skills.
4. Aid creates links between the North (developed countries) and the South (developing countries). This promotes international understanding and world peace.

DISADVANTAGES OF INTERNATIONAL AID

1. Tied aid may benefit the donor country more than the receiver.
2. Aid may cause the receiver to become dependent on the donor country.
3. Aid may be used as a means to 'cover up' unfair trading practices of the North.

ECONOMIC INEQUALITY IN IRELAND

The eastern region around Dublin is richer than the western region of Connacht.

The Area around Dublin

- This is the most important manufacturing and commercial centre in Ireland. More than 95% of employees work in industry and services.
- High incomes create strong spending power that increases local wealth and brings higher living standards.
- Rainfall is only 1000mm or less, which allows for large-scale cereal and mechanised farming methods. The area is one of rich lowland farmland.
- Land and housing reach very high prices, which has made many people rich in recent years.

West Connacht

- Only 20% of workers are employed in manufacturing and service industries.
- Most other jobs provide low incomes, so people are poorer than in the east.
- Much of the land is covered with high mountains and uplands such as the Twelve Bens and Nephin Mountains.
- Most farms are small and many depend on agriculture for a living. This provides a low income for many people in the rural regions.
- Heavy rains create peaty and podzol soils that are leached and have few minerals.
- Services such as hospitals, discos and social services are few, so many young adults leave the region and migrate to Dublin or other eastern cities and towns.

ECONOMIC INEQUALITY

Notice: **Higher Course only**

INEQUALITY IN ITALY
Reasons Why Northern Italy is Prosperous
1. Northern Italy forms part of the wealthy core area of the EU. Industry and people are attracted to the core.
2. The flood plain of the River Po has deep alluvial soils rich in minerals giving a high agricultural output.
3. Plentiful supplies of natural gas and hydro-electricity encourage the development of industry.
4. There are many well-established industries in the north such as car manufacture in Turin, and iron and steel manufacture in Genoa.

Reasons Why Southern Italy is not Developed
1. Much of southern Italy is mountainous with only narrow coastal plains available for agriculture.
2. Soils are shallow and dry, so scorching heat in summer gives a low agricultural output.
3. There are very few raw materials located in the south. This hinders industrial development.
4. Roads, services and community facilities are limited due to its isolated position. People migrate from the region.

How has Government Influence Helped the South?
1. Land reform: large estates were divided between peasant farmers.
2. Services: irrigation schemes were developed to bring water to new farms. Agricultural output was improved.
3. Transport: motorways (**autostrada**) were built to remove the isolation of the south.
4. Industry: state-controlled industry was forced to invest 60% of new investment in the south; growth centres were established to encourage the development of industry.

CHAPTER 12   LOCATION GEOGRAPHY

Fig 12.1 Rivers of Ireland

Use the spaces provided to name the rivers 1–26.

1 ....   8 ....   15 ....   22 ....
2 ....   9 ....   16 ....   23 ....
3 ....   10 ....   17 ....   24 ....
4 ....   11 ....   18 ....   25 ....
5 ....   12 ....   19 ....   26 ....
6 ....   13 ....   20 ....
7 ....   14 ....   21 ....

Location Geography

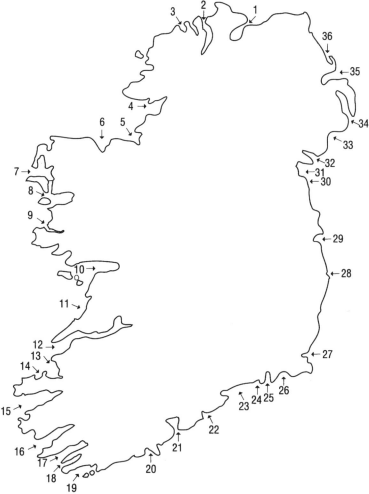

Fig 12.2 Bays and inlets of Ireland

Use the spaces provided to name the bays and inlets 1–36.

1	10	19	28 ....
2	11	20	29 ....
3	12	21	30 ....
4	13	22	31 ....
5	14	23	32 ....
6	15	24	33 ....
7	16	25	34 ....
8	17	26	35 ....
9	18	27	36 ....

Location Geography

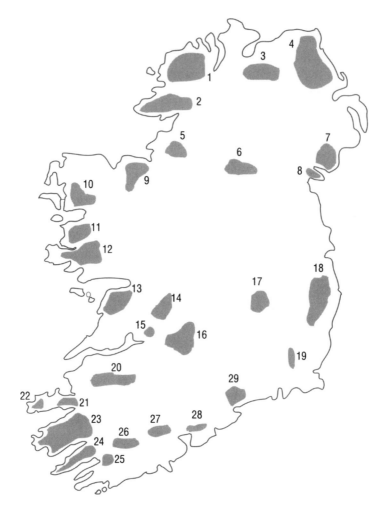

Fig 12.3 Mountains of Ireland

Use the spaces provided to name the mountains 1–29.

1	9	17	25 ....
2	10	18	26 ....
3	11	19	27 ....
4	12	20	28 ....
5	13	21	29 ....
6	14	22	
7	15	23	
8	16	24	

LOCATION GEOGRAPHY

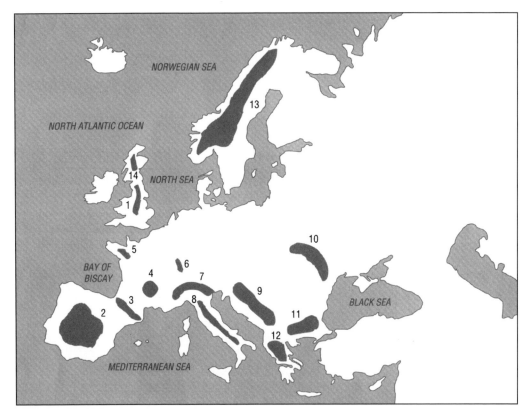

Fig 12.4 Mountains of Europe

Use the spaces provided to name the mountains 1–14.

1 ....   5 ....   9 ....   13 ....
2 ....   6 ....   10 ....   14 ....
3 ....   7 ....   11 ....
4 ....   8 ....   12 ....

Location Geography

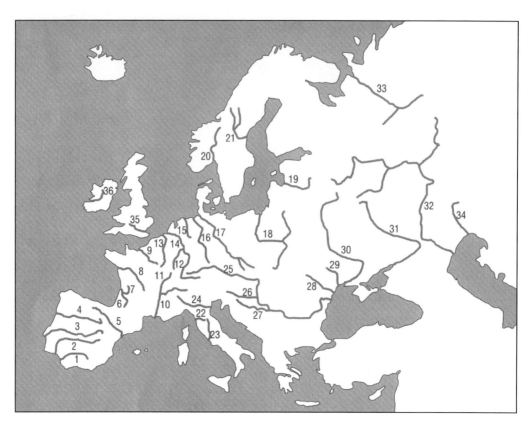

Fig 12.5 Rivers of Europe

Use the spaces provided to name the rivers 1–36.

1	10	19	28 ....
2	11	20	29 ....
3	12	21	30 ....
4	13	22	31 ....
5	14	23	32 ....
6	15	24	33 ....
7	16	25	34 ....
8	17	26	35 ....
9	18	27	36 ....

LOCATION GEOGRAPHY

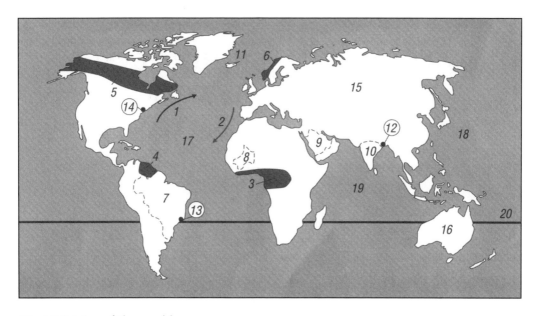

Fig 12.6 Map of the world

Study the map of the world (Fig 12.6) and use the spaces provided to name the following:

Ocean currents	1	*Cities*	12 ....
	2		13 ....
			14 ....
Climates	3		
	4	*Continents*	15 ....
	5		16 ....
	6		
		Oceans	17 ....
Countries	7		18 ....
	8		19 ....
	9		
	10	*Line of latitude*	20 ....
	11		

159

JUNIOR CERTIFICATE EXAMINATION, 2005

GEOGRAPHY – HIGHER LEVEL
SECTION 1 – FOLDER

MONDAY 13th JUNE – AFTERNOON, 1.30 to 3.30

SECTION 1 (60 MARKS)
ALL questions to be answered. You have an either/or choice *within* 3 questions.

1. **CRUSTAL PLATES**

   The map shows some crustal plates and their boundaries.

   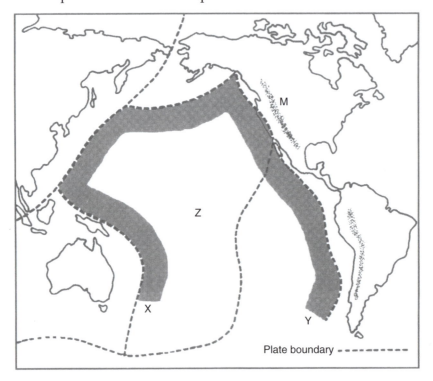

   Circle the correct answer in **each** of the statements below:
   (i) The shaded area labelled **'X–Y'** is *The Pacific Ring of Fire/The Zone of Ice and Fire*.
   (ii) The Plate labelled **'Z'** is *The Nazca Plate/The Pacific Plate*.
   (iii) The Mountains labelled **'M'** are called *The Andes/The Rockies*.

2. **MASS MOVEMENT**

Examine the diagram below.

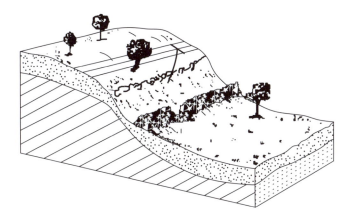

Which type of mass movement does it show?
Tick (✓) the correct box.

Avalanche ☐   Soil Creep ☐

Bog burst ☐   Landslide ☐

3. **RIVER PROCESSES**

The diagrams A, B and C show a river in its upper, middle and lower courses.

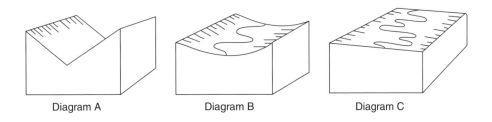

Diagram A   Diagram B   Diagram C

Circle the correct answer in **each** of the statements below:

(i) Sideward erosion is most common in *Diagram A/Diagram B/Diagram C*.

(ii) Deposition is most common in *Diagram A/Diagram B/Diagram C*.

(iii) Downward erosion is most common in *Diagram A/Diagram B/Diagram C*.

EXAMINATION PAPERS

4. **OCEAN CURRENTS**

    The map shows **three** ocean currents of the North Atlantic.

    (i) Name the ocean current labelled A

    _____

    (ii) Name the ocean current labelled B

    _____

    (iii) Say whether the ocean current labelled C is a warm or a cold current.

    _____

5. **DEPRESSION**

    Examine the diagram of a depression given below.

    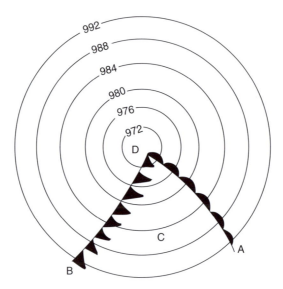

    In the boxes provided match **each** of the labels **A–D** on the diagram with the number of its pair in Column Y. One pair has been completed for you.

Column Y	
1	Cold Front
2	Place of lowest barometric pressure
3	Warm Sector
4	Warm Front

Diagram Label	Y
A	
B	
C	3
D	

EXAMINATION PAPERS

6. THE WATER CYCLE

In the boxes provided match **each** of the terms in **Column X** with its matching pair in **Column Y**. One pair has been completed for you.

	Column X
A	Precipitation
B	Condensation
C	Soakage and run-off
D	Evaporation

	Column Y
1	Results in the formation of cloud
2	Returns water to the sea
3	Water changes into a gas
4	Includes rain, hail, sleet and snow

X	Y
A	
B	
C	
D	3

7. SOIL TYPES

Examine the map below.

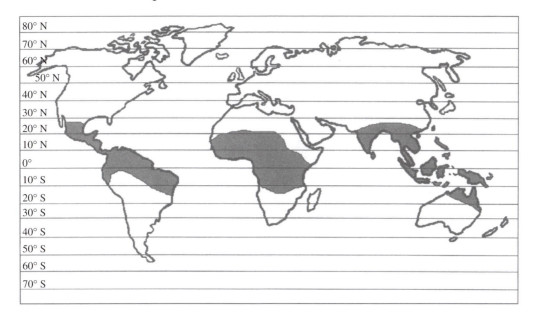

The soil type in the shaded areas of the map is:
Tick (✓) the correct box.

Podzols ☐

Gleys ☐

Brown Soils ☐

Tropical Red Soils ☐

163

EXAMINATION PAPERS

8. **A EUROPEAN COUNTRY**

Examine the map of a European country.

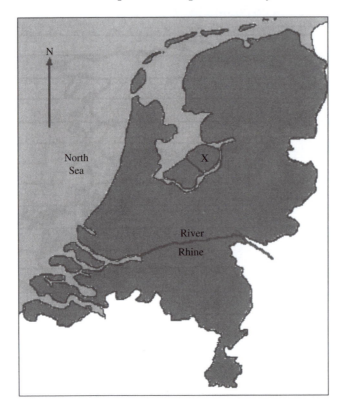

Indicate whether **each** of the statements below is true or false by circling the 'True' or 'False' option.

(i) The country shown is Belgium. *True/False*

(ii) The area labelled '**X**' is an example of a polder. *True/False*

(iii) The River Rhine flows generally westwards through the country. *True/False*

9. **DEMOGRAPHIC TRANSITION (POPULATION CYCLE)**

Examine the diagram (on the next page). Then read the statements below. Not all the statements are true.

1. The diagram shows that birth rates are always higher than death rates.

2. The diagram shows that population growth is slow during Stage 1.

3. The diagram shows that population is decreasing during Stage 5.
4. The diagram shows a rapid fall in birth rates during Stage 1.
5. The diagram shows that population growth is rapid during Stage 2.

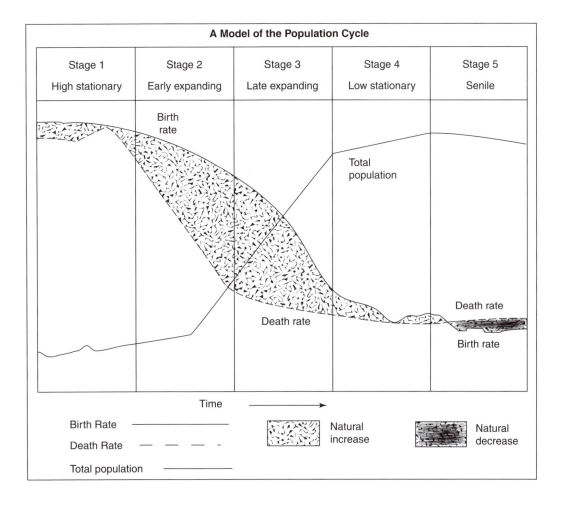

The correct statements are:
Tick (✓) the correct box:
1, 2, 4 ☐   2, 3, 5 ☐
2, 3, 4 ☐   3, 4, 5 ☐

10. URBAN GEOGRAPHY

Indicate whether **each** of the statements below is true or false by circling the *'True'* or *'False'* option.

(i) A **primate city** has at least twice the population of any other city in a country. *True/False*

(ii) A **bustee** is a slum area in a city of a developing country. *True/False*

(iii) **Commuters** are people who travel long distances to work every day. *True/False*

11. URBAN FUNCTIONAL ZONES

The sketch map contains four labelled, functional zones in an imaginary large town in Ireland.

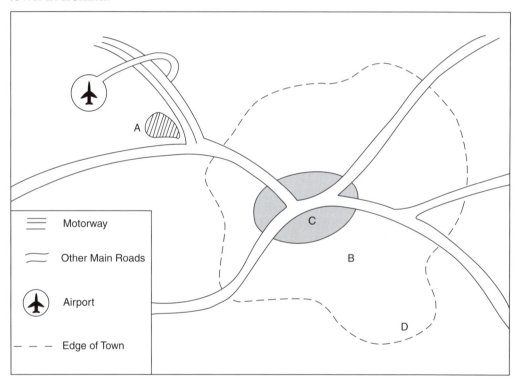

Match **each** of the labels **A–D** on the map with its matching pair from the four Function Zones listed in the table below. One pair has been completed for you.

Functional Zone	Matching label (letter)
C.B.D.	
Older residential (housing) area	
New residential area	
Industrial Estate	A

12. ECONOMIC ACTIVITIES

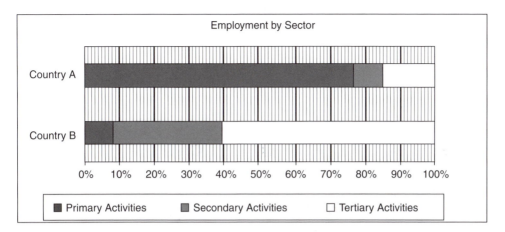

The diagram shows percentage employment by sector in Country A (a slowly developing country) and Country B (a developed country). The statements below relate to the diagrams. Not all of the statements are correct.

1. Most workers in Country A are employed in primary activities.
2. Secondary activities employ more than 10% of workers in Country A.
3. Secondary and tertiary activities combined employ more than 90% of the workforce in Country B.
4. Secondary activities alone employ a greater percentage of workers in Country B than do secondary and tertiary activities together in Country A.
5. Secondary activities employ 39% of the workforce in Country B.

The **correct** statements are:
Tick (✓) the correct box:

1, 3, 4 ☐   2, 3, 4 ☐

1, 3, 5 ☐   3, 4, 5 ☐

13A. CLIMATE

Examine the Table of Figures, which relate to temperature and precipitation at Caherciveen, Co. Kerry.

Month	J	F	M	A	M	J	J	A	S	O	N	D
Temperature (°C)	5	7	9	11	12	14	15	16	14	11	9	6
Precipitation (mm)	92	117	56	19	45	35	23	20	40	75	98	102

EXAMINATION PAPERS

(i) What is the mean monthly temperature for the months of December, January and February together?

(ii) Name the month which has the least precipitation.

OR

13B. MEASURING WATER

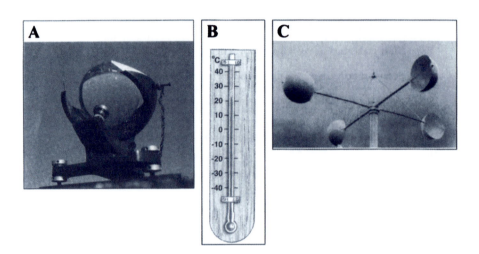

Examine the weather instruments labelled A, B and C.
Read the statements below. Not all of the statements are correct.

1. The instrument labelled A is a barometer.
2. The instrument labelled B is used to measure temperature.
3. The instrument labelled B is kept usually in a Stevenson Screen.
4. The instrument labelled C is an anemometer and measures wind speed.
5. The instrument labelled C is a wind vane and measures wind speed.

The correct statements are:
Tick (✓) the correct box:

1, 2, 4   ☐   2, 3, 4   ☐
2, 3, 5   ☐   3, 4, 5   ☐

EXAMINATION PAPERS

14A. MIXED FARMING AS A SYSTEM

Which of the following might **all** be **outputs** of an Irish mixed farm:
Tick (✓) the correct box:

Barley, tractor, chickens, eggs ☐

Milk, silage, grass, manure ☐

Potatoes, barley, labour, land ☐

Farm buildings, calves, silage, wool ☐

OR

14B. MIXED FARMING LAND USE

The information in the **table** and **pie chart** shows the % areas given over to different land uses in a mixed farm in Ireland.
Complete the pie chart by writing in the name of **each** crop in its correct box.

Crop	% Area
Grass	55
Wheat	20
Sugar beet	10
Barley	10
Potatoes	5

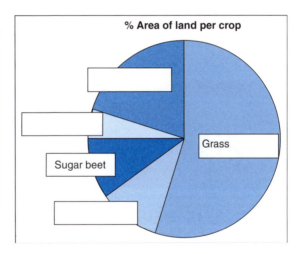

15A. MANUFACTURING INDUSTRY

In the boxes provided, match **each** letter in **Column X** with the number of its pair in **Column Y**. One pair has been completed for you.

	Column X		Column Y	X	Y
A	Capital	1	Industry which can locate in a wide range of places	A	4
B	Footloose	2	Iron and steel making	B	
C	Heavy Industry	3	Assist industry by helping to improve roads, etc.	C	
D	Structural Funds	4	Money needed to set up or run an industry	D	

OR

169

EXAMINATION PAPERS

15B. INDUSTRIAL LOCATION

The British iron and steel industry changed its location over time:
Tick (✓) the correct box.

From coasts to coalfields ☐
From coalfields to forested areas ☐
From coalfields to coasts ☐
From coasts to forested areas ☐

16. STREET MAP

Examine the street map, which shows part of Central Dublin.

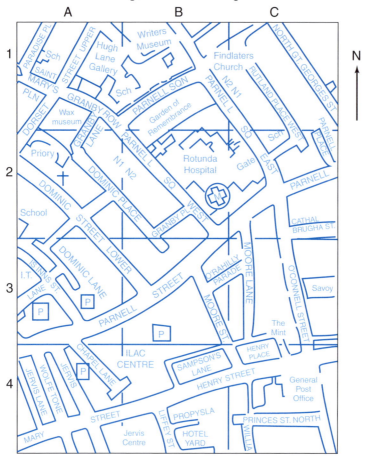

Imagine that you are asked to take the following journey:
- Walk along Parnell Sq. West (grid B2) in a south-easterly direction.
- Then turn right along Parnell Street in a south-westerly direction.
- Then enter the street on the second turn to your left.

On which street would you then find yourself?
Tick (✓) the correct box.

Dominic Street Lower	☐	O'Rahilly Parade	☐
Parnell Place	☐	Chapel Lane	☐

17. AERIAL PHOTOGRAPH

Study the Aerial Photograph supplied.
Circle the correct answer in **each** of the statements below.

- The trees in the right background are mainly *coniferous/deciduous*.
- The waterway in the left background is *a river/a canal*.
- The photograph was most likely taken in *winter/summer*.

18. ORDNANCE SURVEY

Study the Ordnance Survey map and legend (key) supplied.

In the boxes provided, match **each** letter in **Column X** with the number of its pair in **Column Y**. One pair has been completed for you.

Column X			Column Y		X	Y
A	N 401 541	1	Crannóg		A	
B	N 453 553	2	Nature reserve		B	
C	N 448 568	3	Lake		C	
D	N 426 587	4	Earthwork		D	2

19. ORDNANCE SURVEY

Study the Ordnance Survey map and legend (key) supplied.

The **direction** from the Picnic Site at N 420 585 to the Nature Reserve at N 426 587 is:
Tick (✓) the correct box.

North East	☐	North West	☐
South East	☐	South West	☐

* For Ordnance Survey map and photograph see pages 179–80 of this book, and for key see page 181.

EXAMINATION PAPERS

20. ORDNANCE SURVEY

This rural settlement pattern within the grid square N 40 53 is:
Tick (✓) the correct box.

Mainly Linear ☐ Mainly Dispersed ☐
Mainly Nucleated ☐ Partly Dispersed and Partly Nucleated ☐

JUNIOR CERTIFICATE EXAMINATION, 2005

GEOGRAPHY – HIGHER LEVEL

MONDAY 13th JUNE – AFTERNOON, 1.30 to 3.30

SECTION 2 (90 MARKS)
Answer **THREE** questions.

1. CLIMATE AND TOURISM

A. *'Altitude and Aspect can each affect the local climate of an area.'*

Examine the diagram below and answer the questions which follow.

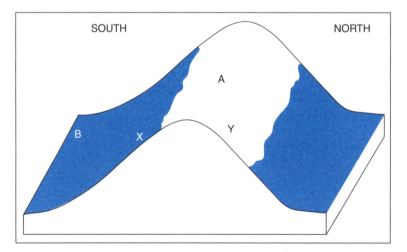

(i) Explain **one** reason why the place labelled **A** is likely to be colder than the place labelled **B**.

(ii) Explain **one** reason why the place labelled **X** is likely to be warmer than the place labelled **Y**. (8)

EXAMINATION PAPERS

B. 'Climate makes some regions attractive to tourists.'

Examine the graphs below, which show the precipitation and temperature figures for a popular tourist region in Europe. Answer the questions which follow.

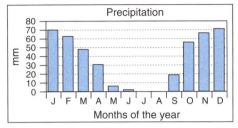
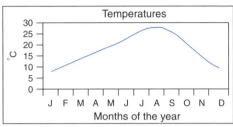

(i) Describe **two** ways in which the climate shown would attract tourists.

(ii) Name the type of climate.

(iii) Name **one** country in Europe where this climate may be found. (10)

C. 'Large-scale tourism can cause major problems for busy tourist regions.'

Describe **three** problems associated with large-scale tourism. (12)

2. SETTLEMENT AND URBAN PLANNING

A. Explain how any **two** of the following influence population densities throughout the world:

- Soils
- Relief (shape of the land surface)
- Mineral Wealth (8)

B. Examine the map below, which shows part of Northern Africa.

Answer the questions which follow.

The country labelled **X** on the map has a very low human population density.

(i) Name the country labelled **X**.

(ii) Describe **two** problems **caused by** low population density which affect the country labelled **X** on the map. (10)

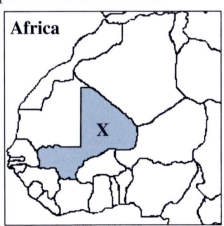

C. *'Urban Renewal, Urban Redevelopment and New Towns are all used by planners to reduce problems of modern city life.'*

(i) Examine the newspaper extract provided here and state whether it refers to Urban Renewal or to Urban Redevelopment.

Dublin Corporation is trying to persuade people in parts of the old Liberties area of the inner city not to abandon their old neighbourhoods. With this in mind, many houses are being restored by the Corporation and new community services are being provided in the area.

(ii) Briefly describe **one** difference between Urban Renewal and Urban Redevelopment.

(iii) Name **any** New Town in Ireland.

(iv) Briefly describe **two** typical features of this New Town. (12)

3. NATURAL RESOURCES AND PEOPLE

A. Examine Picture A and Picture B, which show two different **rock types** in Ireland. Answer the questions which follow.

Picture A - The Giant's Causeway

Picture B - The Burren

(i)
- Name the rock type shown in **Picture A** and the rock type shown in **Picture B**.
- Indicate whether **each** of the rock types you name is igneous, sedimentary or metamorphic.

(ii) Describe **two** ways in which rocks may be of economic use to people. (12)

B. Look again at Picture **B** of the Burren. Explain fully how rainwater weathers the rock shown in this picture. (8)

EXAMINATION PAPERS

C. Examine the graph, which shows that **fish stocks** have become depleted over time in part of the Irish Sea. Answer the questions which follow.

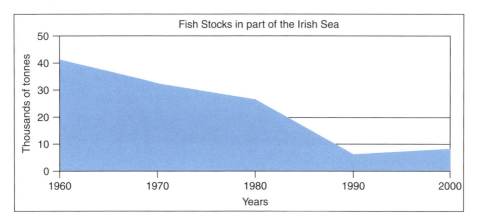

(i) Calculate the decrease in fish stocks shown between 1960 and 1990.

(ii) Describe **two** possible reasons for the depletion in fish stocks in the seas around Ireland. (10)

4. GEOGRAPHICAL MIX

Answer ANY THREE of the questions A–D below.

A. Answer **EITHER** the questions on **Sea Erosion OR** the questions on **Glacial Erosion**.

Sea Erosion

Examine the diagram showing some coastal features. Answer the questions which follow.

(i) Name the **four** features of sea erosion labelled **1–4** on the diagram.

(ii) Describe **two** processes (two ways) by which waves erode the coast.

(10)

OR

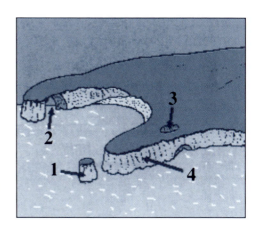

Glacial Erosion

Examine the diagram showing some glacial features. Answer the questions which follow.

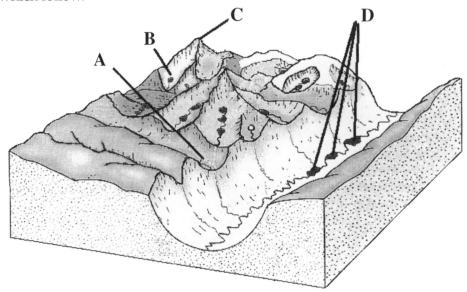

(i) Name the **four** glacial features labelled **A–D** on the diagram.

(ii) Describe **two** processes (two ways) by which moving ice has eroded the landscape. (10)

B. Population Pyramids

Examine the population pyramids labelled **Country A** and **Country B**. One pyramid shows the population structure of a developing country and the other shows the population structure of a developed country. Answer the questions that follow.

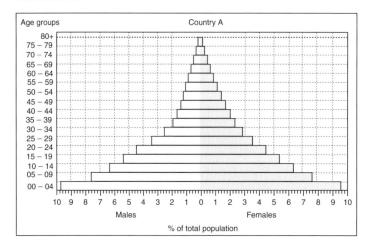

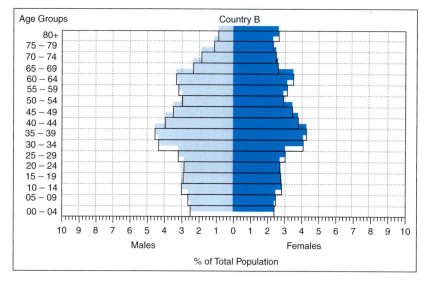

(i) Which country, **A** or **B**, is a developed country?

(ii) Explain **why** the population structures of developing countries and developed countries are so different under the following headings:
- Birth rates
- Death rates
- Life expectancy (10)

C. **Organised Migration**

(i) Name **one** example of organised international migration.
(ii) Describe **two** reasons why this organised migration took place.
(iii) Describe **one** long-term effect of this migration in the destination country.
(10)

D. **War, Military Spending and Development**

Explain **two** ways in which war and the spending of money on arms have prevented economic development in **one** named developing country of your choice. (10)

5. **ORDNANCE SURVEY AND AERIAL PHOTOGRAPH**

A. Study the **Ordnance Survey Map** and the legend (key) supplied.

(i) What is the **straight line** distance in **kilometres** from the summit of Frewin Hill [171] at N 377 586 to the Nature Reserve at N 426 587?

(ii) What is the distance in **kilometres** along the **R 394** road from the church at N 437 532 to the church at N 447 584? (6)

B. Using evidence from the **Ordnance Survey Map** only, explain **three** reasons why tourists may be attracted to the area shown on the map. (12)

C. Draw a sketch map of the area shown on the **Aerial Photograph.** Show **and** name the following features:
- **Two** connecting streets
- A church
- A car park
- A section of canal
- A housing estate. (12)

© Peter Barrow Photography

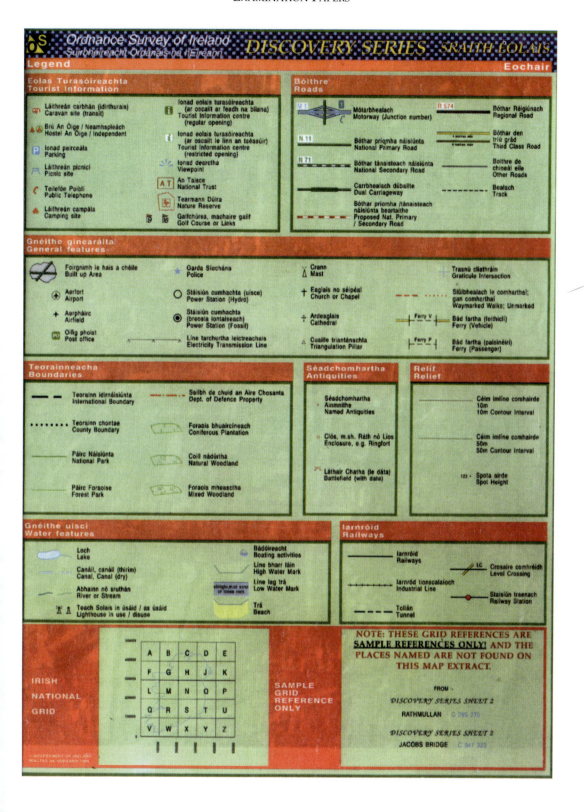

Examination Papers

JUNIOR CERTIFICATE EXAMINATION, 2006

GEOGRAPHY – HIGHER LEVEL
SECTION 1 – FOLDER

MONDAY 12th JUNE – AFTERNOON, 1.30 to 3.30

SECTION 1 (60 MARKS)

1. **CRUSTAL PLATES**

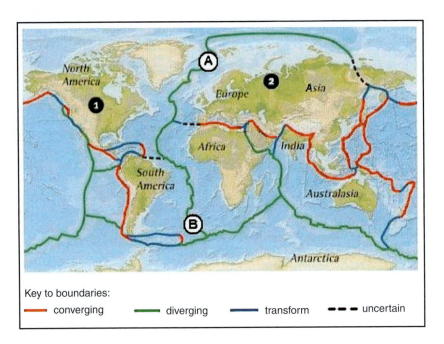

Examine the map showing the world's principal crustal plates.

(i) Name the crustal plate labelled "1"._____

(ii) Name the crustal plate labelled "2"._____

(iii) Name the ocean feature which results from plates separating along the line labelled A–B.

_____

EXAMINATION PAPERS

2. **ROCKS**

   Complete the three-piece crossword using these clues:

   1. Coarse red or brown sedimentary rock found in the mountains of Munster.
   2. A coarse multi-coloured, igneous rock.
   3. Rocks which were changed by great pressure or heat.

3. **MASS MOVEMENT**

   The type of mass movement illustrated in the diagrams is:

   Tick (✓) the correct box.

   Soil Creep ☐

   A Mudflow ☐

   A Landslide ☐

   A Bogburst ☐

   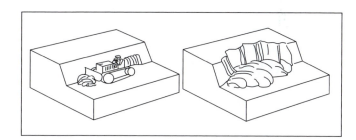

183

4. RIVERS

In the boxes provided, match **each** of the letters **A** to **D** in the diagram with the number of its pair in Column X. One pair has been completed for you.

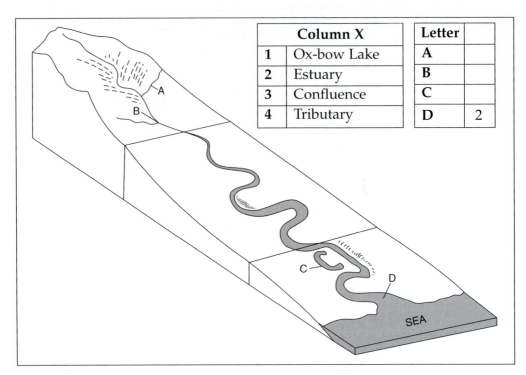

Column X	
1	Ox-bow Lake
2	Estuary
3	Confluence
4	Tributary

Letter	
A	
B	
C	
D	2

5. CLIMATE STATISTICS

Examine the temperature and precipitation statistics for a town in Central Europe

	J	F	M	A	M	J	J	A	S	O	N	D
Temperature (°C)	-4.5	-0.5	2.5	6.0	8.5	12.5	16.0	17.5	12.5	6.5	2.0	-1.0
Precipitation (mm)	11	15	42	36	62	75	99	97	31	32	24	19

Circle the correct answer in **each** of the following statements:

(i) The warmest month is *July / August*.

(ii) The annual temperature range is *22°C / 13°C*.

(iii) A *hygrometer/rain gauge* was used to measure rainfall levels to make this chart.

6. TEMPERATURE MAP

Examine the August temperature map of Ireland.

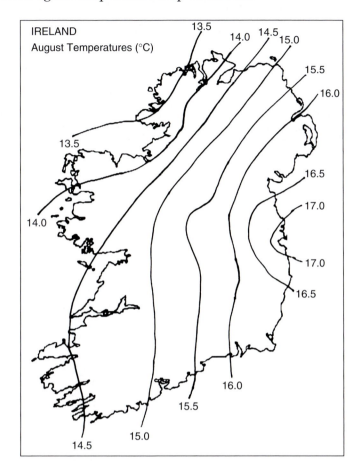

Circle the correct answer in **each** of the following statements.

(i) The coolest part of Ireland is the *north east* / the *north west*.

(ii) The warmest region has a temperature of *just over 17°C* / *just under 17°C*.

(iii) The lines on the map joining places of equal temperature are called *isobars* / *isotherms*.

7. POPULATION CHANGE

Examine the diagram showing the population cycle.

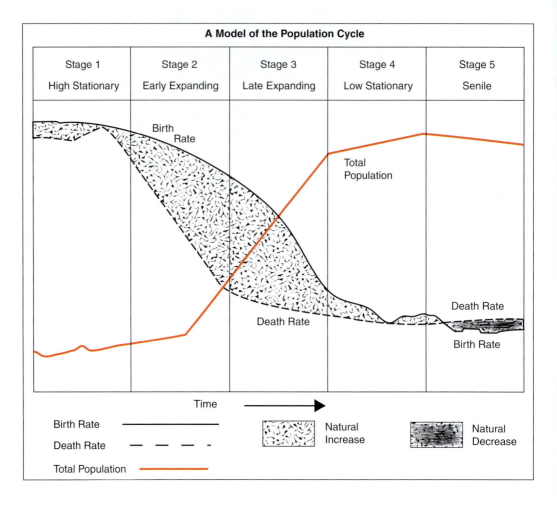

(i) At which of the five stages shown is the death rate highest? _____

(ii) At which of the five stages is the total population increasing most rapidly? _____

(iii) At which of the five stages is there an overall decrease in the total population? _____

8. POPULATION STRUCTURE

Examine the diagram, which represents the structure of the population of a small urban area.

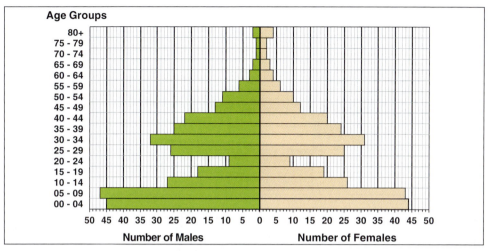

(i) How many males are there in the 0–4 age group?_____

(ii) This diagram represents an area where *young families/very old people* make up most of the population. (*Circle the correct option.*)

(iii) What name is given to this type of diagram?_____

9. GRAPH DRAWING

The bars represent the information given in the table of figures. Draw in the bars for Belgium, Ireland and Poland.

Table of figures	
Expected population change between 2004 and 2050 in a number of countries.	
Country	*Percentage change*
Belgium	+5
France	+10
Italy	-9
Ireland	+36
Netherlands	+7
Poland	-12
United Kingdom	+8
(Source: Irish Times, 9 April 2005)	

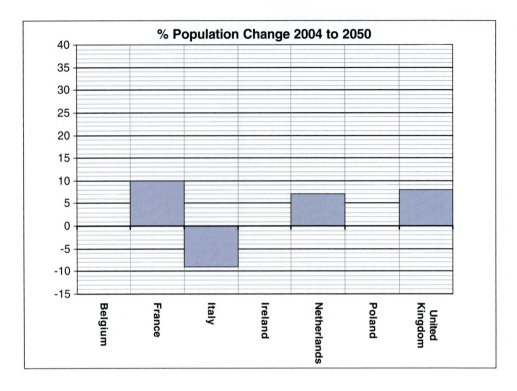

10. SETTLEMENT

In the boxes provided match **each** letter in Column X with the number of its pair in Column Y. One pair has been completed for you.

	Column X
A	Tallaght
B	Mali
C	Polders
D	Bustees

	Column Y
1	Land reclaimed from the sea
2	Shanty towns
3	New town
4	Low population density

X	Y
A	3
B	
C	
D	

EXAMINATION PAPERS

11. FUNCTIONAL ZONES WITHIN CITIES

Study the sketch map showing some functional zones within a city.

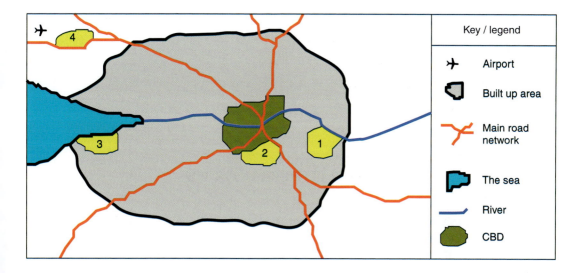

In the boxes provided, match **each** of the numbers **1** to **4** in the sketch map with the letter of its pair in Column X. One pair has been completed for you.

	Column X
A	Dockside Industries
B	Older Residential Area
C	Modern Industrial Estate
D	Newer Residential Area

X	Number
A	
B	
C	
D	1

12. ASPECTS OF SETTLEMENT

Read the statements below. Not all of the statements are true.

1. Dolmens, ring forts and castles are all signs of former settlement.

2. A village which clusters around a road junction has a ribboned settlement pattern.

3. The West of Ireland is more densely populated than the East of Ireland.

4. Land values usually increase towards the centre of a city.

5. The River Rhine flows through Germany but enters the sea in the Netherlands.

The correct statements are numbered:
Tick (✓) the correct box.

1, 4, 5 ☐

1, 3, 4 ☐

2, 3, 4 ☐

2, 4, 5 ☐

ANSWER EITHER 13A OR 13B

13A. EXPLOITING IRELAND'S PEAT BOGS

Circle the correct answer in **each** of the following statements:

(i) Drains are dug in the bogs by machines called *drainers/ditchers*.

(ii) Small amounts of peat are scraped off the bogs and torn up into small fragments by machines called *graders/millers*.

(iii) In bygone days, hand tools called *sleans/harrows* were used to cut sods of turf from the bog.

OR

13B. PRIMATE CITIES

A primate city
Tick (✓) the correct box.

Is the city in which a country's parliament meets. ☐

Is the oldest city in a country. ☐

Is a place from which people commute to and from work each day. ☐

Has at least twice the human population of any other city in a country. ☐

EXAMINATION PAPERS

ANSWER EITHER 14A OR 14B

14A. SOIL

Choose **three terms** from the selection box to fill the gaps in the extract below.

Selection Box.
Leaching; Micro-organisms; Humus; Mineral particles; Podzols; Hard pans

The breakdown of plant litter into _____ helps to fertilise soil. Processes such as _____ may damage soil fertility by causing nutrients to seep below the reach of plant roots. _____ are a type of soil commonly found in damp highland areas in Ireland.

OR

14B. SOIL

The divided bar chart shows the composition of soil.

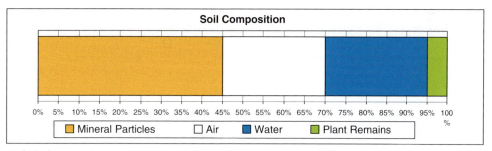

Label the pie-chart, using the information on the divided bar.

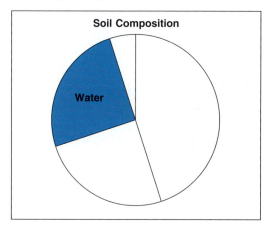

ANSWER EITHER 15A OR 15B

15A. THE WATER CYCLE

Study the diagram of the water cycle.

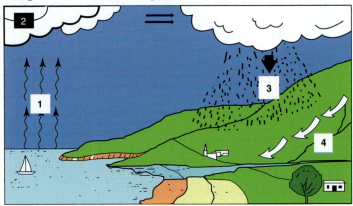

In the boxes provided match **each** of the numbers **1** to **4** in the diagram with the letter of its pair in Column X. One pair has been completed for you.

	Column X
A	Precipitation
B	Condensation
C	Run off and Soakage
D	Evaporation

	Number
A	
B	2
C	
D	

OR

15B. TYPES OF RAINFALL

Study the diagram below

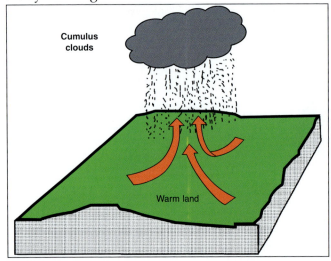

The diagram shows

Tick (✓) the correct box.

Relief Rainfall ☐

Convectional Rainfall ☐

Cyclonic/Frontal Rainfall ☐

16. THE THIRD WORLD

Examine the information given about the Third World.

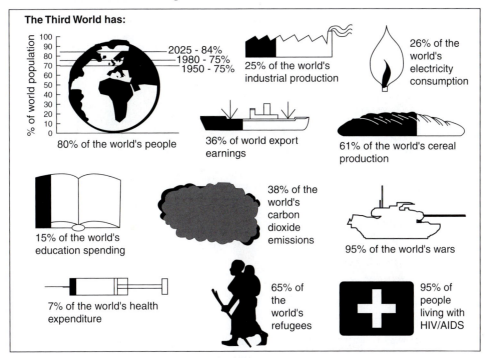

Read the statements below. Not all of the statements are true.
Identify the true statements by *ticking (✓) the correct box*.

1. The Third World has more than three quarters of the world's people.
2. Most of the world's carbon dioxide emissions come from the Third World.
3. The Third World has less than one-tenth of the world's health expenditure.
4. Most of the world's cereal production is in the Third World.
5. 36% of the world's industrial production is in the Third World.

The true statements are

1, 2, 3 ☐

2, 3, 4 ☐

1, 3, 4 ☐

3, 4, 5 ☐

17. HUNGER AND PLENTY

The map shows average daily calorie intakes in different countries.

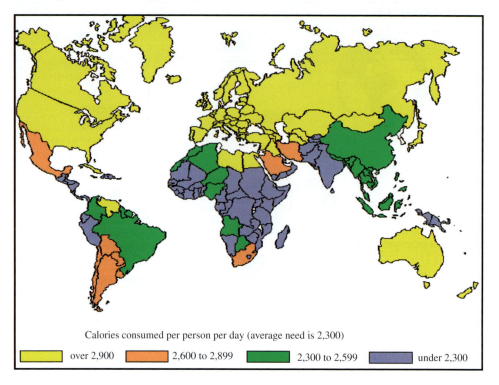

Write the daily calorie intake per person in **each** of the following countries:

In Ireland_____

In Brazil_____

In Mali_____

EXAMINATION PAPERS

18. ORDNANCE SURVEY - SLOPES

In the boxes provided, match **each** letter in Column X with the number of its pair in Column Y.
One pair has been completed for you.

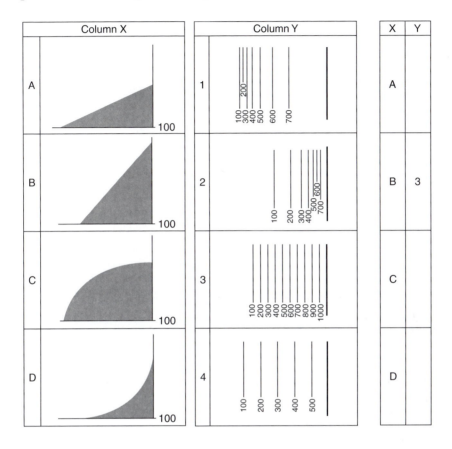

19. ORDNANCE SURVEY – GRID REFERENCES

Study the ORDNANCE SURVEY map provided (page 197).

In the boxes provided, match each letter in column X with the number of its pair in column Y.
One pair has been completed for you.

Column X	
A	V 957 856
B	V 933 927
C	V 959 908
D	V 908 923

Column Y	
1	Cathedral
2	Devil's Island
3	Caravan Site
4	Viewpoint

X	Y
A	2
B	
C	
D	

20. ORDNANCE SURVEY - AREA

Examine the ORDNANCE SURVEY map provided with this examination (page 197).

Lough Leane has an approximate area of.

Tick (✓) the appropriate box

14 square kilometres ☐

18 square kilometres ☐

22 square kilometres ☐

25 square kilometres ☐

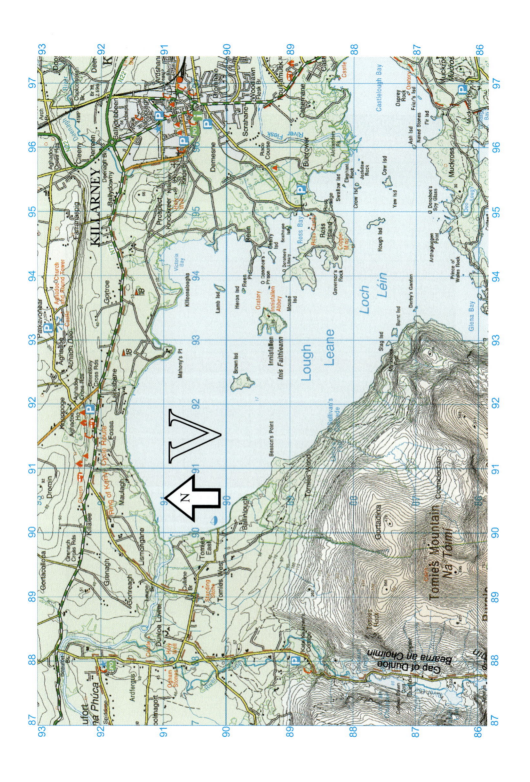

Examination Papers

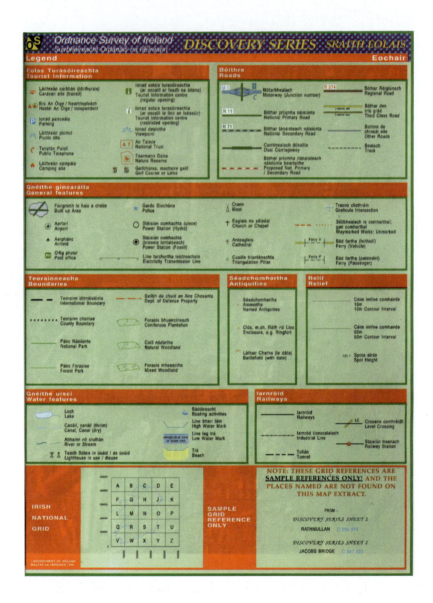

EXAMINATION PAPERS

JUNIOR CERTIFICATE EXAMINATION, 2006

GEOGRAPHY – HIGHER LEVEL

MONDAY 12th JUNE – AFTERNOON, 1.30 to 3.30

SECTION 2 (90 MARKS)
Answer **THREE** questions.

1. **WEATHER, TOURISM AND INDUSTRIAL ACTIVITIES**

A. **Irish Weather**

The **weather chart** shows a large cyclone or depression over Ireland.

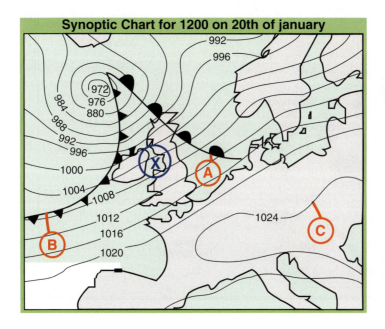

(i) Name **each** of the features labelled **A, B** and **C** on the chart.

(ii) Describe the weather conditions which you would expect to find in the area labelled **X** on the chart. Refer briefly in your answer to atmospheric pressure, cloud and precipitation. (9)

B. **Climate and Tourism**

"Climate helps to make some parts of Europe attractive to tourists."

Explain this statement, referring to **one** European country or region which you have studied. (11)

C. **Acid Rain**

(i) Explain how industrial activities can cause acid rain.

The map shows clusters of manufacturing industry and acid rain levels in Western Europe.

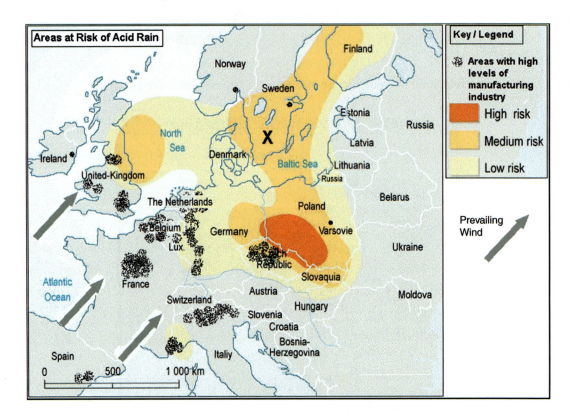

(ii) The area labelled X on the map is lightly populated and is not heavily industrialised.

Suggest then why the area labelled X suffers from high levels of acid rain.

(10)

EXAMINATION PAPERS

2. NATURAL RESOURCES, PROCESSES AND PEOPLE

A. Weathering in the Burren

The photograph shows the surface of part of the Burren region in Co. Clare.

(i) **Name** the type of rock which occurs in the area shown.

(ii) **Describe** fully the type of weathering that takes place in the area shown.

(8)

B. Hydroelectric Scheme

The photograph shows a dam and hydroelectric station on an Irish river.

(i) Name **one** economic benefit **and one** environmental benefit of hydroelectricity.

(ii) Outline **two** objections which might be made to the development of a hydroelectric scheme such as the one shown. (10)

201

EXAMINATION PAPERS

C. Depletion of a natural resource

The table of figures shows change over time in herring catches in part of the Celtic Sea off Ireland. (*Catch given in thousands of tonnes*)

YEAR	ANNUAL CATCH*	YEAR	ANNUAL CATCH*	YEAR	ANNUAL CATCH*
1970	26.7	1980	6.3	1990	12.2
1971	24.9	1981	6.4	1991	11.9
1972	23.4	1982	6.8	1992	13.7
1973	22.6	1983	7.1	1993	10.4
1974	19.3	1984	7.5	1994	8.2
1975	17.2	1985	7.9	1995	7.6
1976	13.6	1986	10.0	1996	6.2
1977	11.0	1987	11.7	1997	6.0
1978	10.7	1988	12.0	1998	6.5
1979	6.7	1989	11.9	1999	6.6

(i) To what extent does the table of figures show that fish stocks have been depleted over time in the seas off Ireland?

(ii) Describe **three** reasons for the depletion of fish stocks in Irish waters. (12)

3. INEQUALITIES

A. Life expectancy and child mortality rates

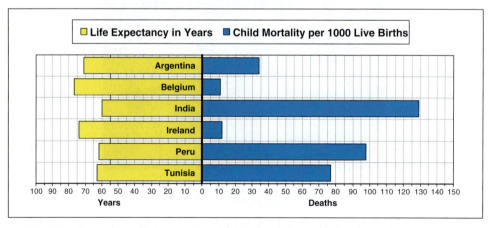

Judging by the information given in the graphs above:

(i) Which of the countries named is the most developed?

(ii) Which of the countries named is the least developed?

(iii) Give **two** reasons why life expectancy is higher in countries of the First World (the North) than it is in countries of the Third World (the South).

(8)

B. Cities of the South

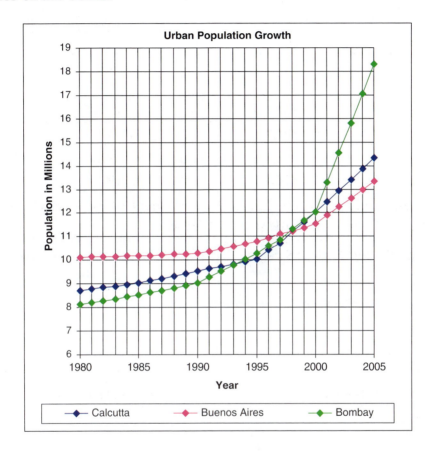

Examine the line graphs, which show population growth in three large Third World cities:

(i) Rank these cities 1, 2 and 3 according to their rate of population growth. (Rank the city with the most rapid population growth as 1.)

(ii) In which year did Bombay overtake Buenos Aires in population?

(iii) In the case of **any one** Third World city which you have studied, describe **two** problems resulting from rapid population growth.

(12)

C. Inequalities within European states

Study the map which shows some Richer and Poorer Regions in Europe:

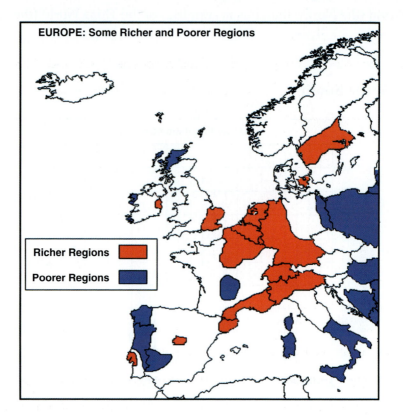

(i) Name **two** poorer regions shown on the map.

(ii) In the case of **one** of the named poorer regions, describe **two** reasons why it is poor.

(10)

4. GEOGRAPHICAL MIX

Answer ANY THREE of the questions A - D below.

A. The growth of cities

The two maps show the growth of Dublin between 1936 and 1988.

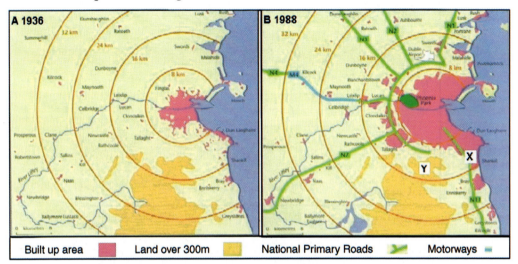

(i) With reference to one or both of the maps:

- Suggest **one** reason for the rapid growth of Dublin at the place labelled **X**.
- Suggest **one** reason for the less rapid development of Dublin at the place labelled **Y**.

(ii) Describe **two** economic reasons for the growth of **any one** Irish city which you have studied. (10)

B. Aerial Photograph

Study the aerial photograph of Killarney provided (page 208).
Draw a *sketch map* of the area shown on the photograph.
On your sketch map **show and name** the following:

- **Two** connecting streets.
- A large car park
- A church
- A large area of deciduous woodland. (10)

C. **Factors which affect climate**

Examine the map which shows part of Europe:

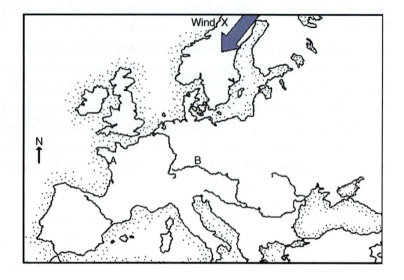

(i) State which of the two places, A or B, has warmer summers and colder winters and explain why.

(ii) Explain how the prevailing wind labelled X would affect the climate of the lands over which it blows. (10)

D. **Human Migration**

(i) Explain the meanings of **each** of the following terms which relate to human migration:

- Push factors of migration
- Pull factors of migration
- Barriers to migration

EXAMINATION PAPERS

Read the passage below

> When Brid Ní Laoghaire left her West Kerry home in 1851 there was barely enough to eat. Following the death of her husband in a fishing accident off the Great Blasket Island, Brid had no option but to follow her eldest sister Maire to Boston. It was Maire who made Brid's trip possible by sending the fare – a small fortune of nine pounds – for Brid to sail to Boston from Queenstown in the County of Cork. Saying goodbye to her ageing parents would be the hardest part of Brid's going; though she was encouraged by the prospects of a job as a kitchen maid in the same house in which Maire had reached the elevated post of assistant housekeeper. On the night before her departure an "American wake" was held in Brid's homestead outside Ballyferriter. Then another daughter of Erin joined the ever-growing exodus to a foreign land.
> From *An Irish Emigrant's Story*

(ii) Identify **one** example of a **push factor**, **one** example of a **pull factor** and **one** example of a **barrier** to migration, each of which is mentioned in the passage above.

(iii) Name one other barrier to migration, which is not mentioned in the passage. (10)

5. **ORDNANCE SURVEY MAP AND AERIAL PHOTOGRAPH**

   A. What is the direction from Brown Isd. (V 923 897) to Cow Isd. (V 955 874) on the **O.S. map** (page 197)? (3)

   B. Explain why there is little or no settlement at **each** of the following places on the **O. S. map**:
      - At V 89 88
      - At V 961 891 (6)

   C. Referring to the **O.S. map** explain **two** different reasons why Killarney and its surrounding countryside is a popular tourist area. (12)

   D. Examine the **aerial photograph** (page 208). Imagine that it was proposed to build a computer factory in the field on the extreme right background of the photograph. Do you think that this is a suitable area for such a factory? Give **two** arguments to support your answer. Refer to the photograph in your arguments. (9)